I0104962

Quarterly Essay

Quarterly Essay is published four times a year by Black Inc., an imprint of Schwartz Media Pty Ltd. Publisher: Morry Schwartz.

ISBN 978-1-86395-466-2 ISSN 1832-0953

Subscriptions – 1 year (4 issues): $49 within Australia incl. GST. Outside Australia $79.
2 years (8 issues): $95 within Australia incl. GST. Outside Australia $155.
Payment may be made by Mastercard or Visa, or by cheque made out to Schwartz Media. Payment includes postage and handling.

To subscribe, fill out and post the subscription card, or subscribe online at:

www.quarterlyessay.com

Correspondence and subscriptions should be addressed to the Editor at:

Black Inc. Level 5, 289 Flinders Lane
Melbourne VIC 3000 Australia
Phone: 61 3 9654 2000 / Fax: 61 3 9654 2290
Email:
quarterlyessay@blackincbooks.com (editorial)
subscribe@blackincbooks.com (subscriptions)

Editor: Chris Feik. Management: Sophy Williams, Caitlin Yates. Publicity: Elisabeth Young. Design: Guy Mirabella. Production Co-ordinator: Adam Shaw

| WHAT'S RIGHT? | *The Future of Conservatism in Australia* |

Waleed Aly

Andrew Kenny's brilliant essay in the 5 February 2005 issue of the *Spectator* should be made compulsory reading for anyone interested in contemporary political discourse. It is a swift, clinical, devastating demolition of the twin terms that are so relentlessly and unthinkingly used to frame our discussions of politics. Those terms, of course, are Left and Right, and in spite of their ubiquity they are utterly meaningless and should be abandoned by anyone interested in having a substantial political conversation. Here is Kenny's first paragraph:

> Is Osama bin Laden left-wing or right-wing? How about Robert Mugabe? Who has a more left-wing approach to women's sexuality: Pope John Paul or *Hustler* magazine? Consider Fidel Castro. He persecutes homosexuals, crushes trade unions, forbids democratic elections, executes opponents and criminals, is a billionaire in a country of very poor people and has decreed that a member of his family shall succeed him in power. Is Castro left-wing or right-wing? Explain your answer.

The terms Left and Right derive from the French Revolution. In 1791, when the French Legislative Assembly sat, those loyal to the king sat on the right of the chamber. Those who supported the revolution sat on the left. It is a seating pattern that continues to this day in our own parliament. The party in government, being the established power, sits on the right wing; the opposition on the left. But it is lamentable that this historical quirk has so captured our lexicon. Even in revolutionary France it told us nothing about questions of substantive policy. At different times, the Left included socialists and supporters of *laissez-faire* economics. There are many things that are worth importing from France: cheese and fashion, for example. Political nomenclature is not among them.

Kenny raises, then eviscerates, every possible definition one might use to try to give meaning to these terms. Do we say Attila the Hun was right-wing because he was violent and cruel? Lenin outdid him in both respects. Is Lenin to the right of Attila? Is it left-wing to believe in individual freedom – like the right to carry guns? Is it right-wing to believe in economic freedom – like the right to unrestricted freedom of movement across national boundaries to find work? Does the Left believe in centrally planned economies, such as in Nazi Germany and apartheid South Africa? Does the Right believe in free trade, as did Adam Smith and Karl Marx? Is it left-wing to hate capitalism, like Hitler? Is the Left internationalist, like McDonald's and the World Trade Organization? Is the Right racist, like the early communist party of apartheid South Africa, whose motto was "Workers of the World Unite, and Fight for a White South Africa!"?

The point is that these terms do not facilitate thought. They merely "replaced rational argument with a playground division into two gangs who understood nothing clearly except how much they hated each other." That is the crux of the matter. Wherever you encounter Left and Right, you are likely to be encountering political vitriol. You are almost certainly not encountering a discussion of anything substantive.

Our political discourse is drenched in Left and Right because it is so deeply impoverished. Left and Right are the hallmark of a political conversation that is obsessed with *teams* and uninterested in *ideas*. That is the way things tend to proceed in this country: we report politics as though it is sport, and sport as though it is politics. The sports pages are full of ideas – about team development, about long-term recruitment strategies, about philosophies of coaching and the psychology of players. The news pages obsess over winners and losers, over political strategy (but not political thought), and, of course, our commentary is full of Left and Right, good and evil, us and them. Yes, there is good and evil in politics and much in between, but at the heart of it all, even if unconsciously, are ideas. Ideas are the engine of political history. In the long run they matter more than short-term winners and losers. It is in many ways irrelevant which party wins the next election – except perhaps for those barracking for a particular team. It matters far more what ideas they use to govern.

In February 2009, Kevin Rudd offered his analysis of the causes of the global financial crisis in an essay for the *Monthly*. At the core of it was an (emphatically negative) assessment of neo-liberalism – one of the most important ideas of the last thirty years of Western politics. No doubt it was a calculated political tactic, designed to establish in the public's mind that the global recession was to be associated with the Liberal Party. Nevertheless, it was a shock to our political discourse: a prime minister analysing at length what neo-liberal ideas meant in practice, and how they had triggered the near-collapse of the global economy. This is not what politicians have tended to do in recent times. Ours is the age of the soundbite, an age hostile to the public discussion of ideas, especially from those seeking election. It elicited entirely predictable responses. Those on team Right derided it as a shabby piece of work, full of perversions of history and grand, vacuous theorising, while those on team Left hailed it as an incisive, honest and much-needed account of our present predicament.

The Right's criticisms seemed, broadly speaking, to comprise the following: 1) Rudd had contradicted himself by claiming to be a "fiscal conservative" and then rejecting neo-liberalism; 2) Rudd had misdiagnosed the causes of the financial crisis; and 3) Rudd was being inconsistent because the neo-liberal policies of the Howard government were in fact only continuing the economic reforms of the Hawke and Keating governments, which he continued to praise. The last point is undoubtedly correct, the second point is highly debatable, and the first point strikes me as ridiculous. But what none of these responses did was to engage with the idea in question. The critics of the Right were concerned to defend neo-liberalism, apparently accepting that they were irrevocably associated with it. That much was clear. Far less clear was what they thought neo-liberalism actually meant. If the only way to be a fiscal conservative is to be a neo-liberal, then this involves a very odd definition of at least one of those terms. Neo-liberalism is about much more than balancing budgets (though it does support this), and, as it happens, many of the Western political leaders to have been most influenced by neo-liberal thought also left office with extremely large deficits.

There were a handful of notable exceptions. Oliver Marc Hartwich from the Centre for Independent Studies, for example, wrote a lengthy paper in response arguing that Rudd had mischaracterised neo-liberalism. In fact, insisted Hartwich, the kind of commercial behaviour that triggered the financial crisis was caused by the abandonment of neo-liberal thought. In Hartwich's view, neo-liberalism was actually quite close to the very thing Rudd was suggesting as a solution to the financial crisis: a middle path between rampant capitalism and communism. This was a welcome intervention, but overwhelmingly the concept of neo-liberalism itself went unexamined in a frenzy of Left/Right trench warfare.

For Andrew Kenny, the two key political ideas are not Left and Right, but liberalism and socialism. Put simply, these are competing ideas of what – and especially how big – the State's role should be in economic and social affairs. Socialists want an activist State, liberals want a limited one. These are certainly defining political ideas of the past two centuries, but Kenny makes one more enticing comment in passing: "The term 'conservative' is much more complicated and deserves thoughtful investigation." He's right.

Liberalism/socialism is not the only fundamental division in our politics. Conservative and its opposite, progressive, are critical too.

In the December 2005 issue of *Quadrant*, Tom Switzer and Neil Clark wrote an illuminating criticism of the decision to invade Iraq, describing it as "most un-conservative." The central justification of that invasion, they argued, was to remove a dictator from power and to establish in place of his rule a democratic regime. This was unjustifiable on conservative grounds. Saddam Hussein posed no threat that could not have been handled through a continuing policy of containment, the campaign was always going to be unduly costly in blood and treasure, and conservatives have no business trying to export democracy. And yet, in Australia, conservatives almost without exception supported the war and continued to spruik for it, even after the disastrous consequences became plain. This was, after all, a war launched by the conservative side of politics in the United States, and eagerly followed by its conservative counterpart in Australia. Britain was a different case. It was under the control of Tony Blair's Labour government, and the war was a more comfortable philosophical fit. Blair had long accepted the progressive tradition of humanitarian military intervention. He took Britain into the Balkans conflict for humanitarian reasons and recently stated that he would still have invaded Iraq had he known Saddam had no weapons of mass destruction. But that is not the language of conservatism, which by its nature eschews utopian designs and adopts far more modest and pragmatic approaches to policy. Indeed, in Britain, conservatives were far more likely to oppose the war than either British Labour voters or Australian conservatives. Even in America, there were conservative voices raised in opposition. But in Australia, there was a rigid pro-war consensus.

Switzer and Clark argued that the reason for this was that Australian conservatives had subscribed to American neo-conservatism *en masse*, and it was the neo-conservative ideology that had introduced such unconservative ideas as the export of democracy. British conservatism had been less affected.

The article resonated with me because I had long felt something was amiss with Australian conservatism. For a long time I have been intrigued by the fact that I find myself in agreement with much conservative political philosophy, yet in consistent disagreement with politicians and commentators who call themselves conservatives. As this essay will show, the concept of neo-conservatism has been a crucial one for me in understanding this disjuncture, although I am quite sure Switzer and Clark would recoil from several of my conclusions.

Ours is an age of inverted politics. The Iraq war and the War on Terror show that most clearly. Here, it was conservatives trying to argue for humanitarian intervention, for the implementation of democracy through military force, for sweeping, radical political and legal change. Meanwhile it was those they described as the Left arguing that political systems cannot readily be exported to foreign societies with different histories and traditions, and that we should not be so rash in our resort to political and legal measures that depart so far from well-worn precedents and may have unpredictable consequences. The Left/Right divide was easy to identify in this debate, of course. The conservative/progressive one less so. The same might be said of the liberal/socialist division.

This essay is about conservatism as a political philosophy: where it came from, where it has been recently, and where it might go next. The sharpest focus is on Australia (and for that reason the British, rather than the Russian conservative tradition, will be the starting point), but the nature of ideas is such that they cannot be neatly contained by national borders and often have to be discussed in broad terms. It is definitely not about Right and Left, and those terms will be assiduously avoided in this essay unless they are intended to capture the sense of trench warfare that remains their only intelligible meaning. It is written out of a conviction that conservatism is a rich tradition that is indispensable in the maintenance of a healthy political culture, but out of a fear that it might be disappearing or evolving into something far less enriching. Naturally, some will dispute the very premise of conservatism's worth. It is common in progressive political thought to dismiss conservatism as no more than an excuse for the preservation of privilege and power inequalities. And indeed, it would be naive to assume that conservatives are immune to such motivations. But to take that position is to take a reductive view of conservative political thought and make any serious conversation with conservatism impossible. It leaves conservatism as little more than an enemy to be defeated, rather than a worthwhile philosophical tradition to be engaged. I do not believe such an approach is useful. Nor do I believe it is correct.

My argument necessarily requires us to engage with a host of other ideas along the way: liberalism, neo-conservatism and, of course, neo-liberalism. These have been among the most important ideas in Western politics over the last century, particularly as far as the conservative political tradition is concerned. And particularly in the case of neo-liberalism and neo-conservatism, I will argue that they have done considerable damage.

As it happens, the future of conservatism is a question of great political moment, particularly in Australia. As the closing weeks of 2009 showed, the conservative side of Australian party politics is presently in the midst of an identity crisis. That is not uncommon in political parties only recently ousted from a long term in government, but the nature of the leadership instability in the Liberal Party is close to unprecedented. The extraordinary circumstances that led to Malcolm Turnbull's axing stunned even the most seasoned Canberra correspondent and revealed that there was something more at stake than party leadership. At base, the current struggle within the Liberal Party is one over ideas. This is not an essay about the Liberal Party, but about these ideas. And for that reason, it is necessary to go back to first principles.

IN THE BEGINNING

"What brought Conservatism into existence," wrote Lord Hugh Cecil in 1912, "was the French Revolution." Here, he is referring to the creation of conservatism in a party-political sense, with the establishment of Britain's Conservative party, but it is undeniable that the French Revolution was a formative moment for conservative thought more broadly. It is during this period that its most revered thinker, Edmund Burke, wrote his most celebrated works, which have become canonical in the conservative tradition.

Burke observed the events of 1789 with horror, moved by the extraordinary violence and loss of life of the revolution itself, which continued in the *régime de la terreur* under Jacobin rule when thousands of people were executed for treason. For Burke the revolutionaries spoke "in the *patois* of fraud; in the cant and gibberish of hypocrisy" and had injected a "black and savage atrocity of mind" into the French population, devoid of "common feelings of nature" and "all sentiments of morality and religion." He attacked what he considered to be key revolutionary ideas – absolute liberty, the rights of man, equality and democracy – but his grandest thematic objection was to the simple fact that the revolution was revolutionary: "The very idea of the fabrication of a new government is enough to fill us with disgust and horror," he wrote, insisting that it was far better "to derive all we possess as an *inheritance from our forefathers.*"

Burke was not merely reactionary or nostalgic in saying this. His analysis proceeded from a deeper understanding of human nature and human society. The essential point for Burke was that human society is *organic*. It is something that has evolved slowly and naturally, incorporating the wisdom of generations and gradually leaving behind those things that have proven themselves to be folly. Human beings, he argued, are complex and highly contextual creatures. They do not exist in the abstract, they are not reducible to essential, absolute properties; they are creatures of memory, of social relations and, accordingly, of history and tradition. That is how they make sense of themselves and their worlds. Naturally implicit in this is the importance of culture and cultural continuity, something emphasised later by the Swiss conservative historian Jacob Burckhardt.

It follows, then, that societies are unfathomably complex – far too complex to be grasped by even the most intelligent person. So much about them is intangible and mysterious that they cannot be altered by design in the way one alters a machine. This is why evolved tradition, custom and culture are important: they capture the sorts of intangible wisdoms that philosophy simply cannot. Accordingly, any social change that is dismissive of tradition or believes it can be swept away dangerously misconceives the nature of humans and human society and invites great ruin. Tradition has its own force and wisdom.

This concept of an organic human society was, and remains, conservatism's most central and crucial philosophical insight. Almost every conservative idea can be derived from it, and indeed its implications extend well beyond opposition to the French Revolution. Implicit here is a strong distrust of what Burke called "abstract principle," particularly as a basis for government. Tradition trumps theory:

> We procure reverence to our civil institutions on the principle which
> Nature teaches us to revere individual men: on account of their age,
> and on account of those from whom they are descended. All your
> sophisters cannot produce anything better adapted to preserve a
> rational and manly freedom than the course we have pursued, who
> have chosen our nature rather than our speculations, our breasts
> rather than our inventions, for the great conservatories and maga-
> zines of our rights and privileges.

This is not necessarily to say that theory and insight are evils, just that they provide a poor basis for governing society. Government is not a forum for experimentation. Since the centuries of collective wisdom distilled in custom and tradition are superior to even the most brilliant theorising, the former is crucial to governmental decision-making:

The science of government being, therefore, so practical in itself, and intended for such practical purposes, a matter which requires experience, and even more experience than any person can gain in his whole life, however sagacious and observing he may be, it is with infinite caution that any man ought to venture upon pulling down an edifice which has answered in any tolerable degree for ages with the common purposes of society, or on building it up again without having models and patterns of approved utility before his eyes.

Established institutions are to be cherished and preserved. Hence, conservatism has been historically associated with the preservation of social hierarchies such as the monarchy and, especially, the aristocracy. This was in part a consequence of the conservative opposition to the French Revolution, which was, after all, a revolt against the aristocracy. For such reasons, conservatism is often criticised for justifying and ossifying privilege and oppression in the name of tradition and for being blind to the way continued oppression may give rise to revolutionary consequences. The English political theorist Harold Laski criticised Burke's approach to the French Revolution on these very grounds: Burke, he argued, failed to recognise that the thirst for revolutionary change was itself a product of the repressive traditions and institutions of aristocratic French society, and so was itself in a sense "organic." There is a degree of truth in this, and it is an oversight conservatives are often at risk of committing, but such a criticism masks the very important fact that while conservatism is pro-tradition and definitely pro-stability, it is certainly not *anti-change*. "A state without the means of some change is without the means of its conserva-tion," wrote Burke. This acknowledges exactly Laski's point: that in order for a society to remain stable and continuous, it cannot be resolutely and absolutely stagnant. A State incapable of evolution "might even risk the loss of that part of the constitution which it wished religiously to preserve." Conservatism does not desire atrophy. It accepts the need for change.

But, in accordance with its organic view of society, it requires that change to be as natural and harmonious as possible. This approach is wonderfully expressed by the twentieth-century Tory minister Quintin Hogg in *The Case for Conservatism*:

> Other parties may be wedded to fixed and unalterable theories of the state. For better or worse, the Conservative party is not. Its internal and indispensable role is to criticise and mould the latest heresy of the moment in the name of tradition, as tradition has itself been enriched and moulded by all the transient theories of the past, knowing full well that what seems at one time an unanswerable and cogent system will in the course of years crumble and disappear from view to form part of the rich soil of culture which it will be the duty of future Conservatives to defend.

This is an important point to grasp because it is what distinguishes conservatism from reactionary nostalgia. There is a conservative tradition of reform, too. While overly cautious at times, conservatism has a modest dynamism within it. As Paul Smith said of the conservative Marquis of Salisbury:

> He had a strong enough sense of history to know that it could not be put in reverse. What he fought for was always the maintenance of an existing order, never the restoration of an old, and even the existing order, he realised, must disintegrate in time.

It should come as little surprise, then, that conservatism's early proponents were highly suspicious of ideas we now take for granted. Perhaps the clearest example of this is the case of democracy. Conservatism's aristocratic instincts, and its sympathy with the idea of inherited privilege, made it comfortable with the ancient idea of a governing class. Democracy, by contrast, courted the dangerous prospect of the uneducated and unqualified gaining access to the levers of power. If there was to be suffrage, it should therefore be limited. The working class, with its lack of education and experience in matters of governance, should not vote because, in the words of Sir James Fitzjames Stephen, it would invert "the true and natural relation between wisdom and folly." By submitting government actions to the assent of even the most dim-witted citizens, the practice of government would be unduly frustrated. In particular, governments might be hamstrung when it came to a matter requiring urgent action. This was particularly relevant at the commencement of the industrial revolution, which many conservative thinkers opposed. Industrial society threw up many complex problems, and for conservatives like Thomas Carlyle, "the captainless many" would be incapable of choosing rulers to confront them.

If we take these conservatives at their word – and for the purposes of discerning conservatism's philosophical content, we should – their objections were not motivated merely by a desire to maintain aristocratic power. They were concerned ultimately with good governance. Chiefly, this meant the preservation of liberty and protection from tyranny. These were far from spurious concerns, particularly given the tyranny of the Jacobin regime in France. Here, for instance, is the conservative Irish historian William Lecky:

> To place the chief power in the most ignorant classes is to place it in the hands of those who naturally care least for political liberty, and who are most likely to follow with an absolute devotion some strong leader. The sentiment of nationality penetrates very deeply into all classes; but in all countries and ages it is the upper and middle classes who have chiefly valued constitutional liberty, and those classes it is the work of democracy to dethrone. At the same time democracy does much to weaken among these the love of liberty. The instability and insecurity of democratic politics; the spectacle of dishonest and predatory adventurers climbing by popular suffrage into positions of great power in the State; the alarm which attacks on property seldom fail to produce among those who have something to lose, may easily scare to the side of despotism large

classes who, under other circumstances, would have been steady supporters of liberty.

The conservative fear was that a majoritarian oppression would result, leading to a greater centralisation of political power in government and the erosion of social structures that had previously protected people from persecution. As Alexis de Tocqueville argued upon observing democracy in America, there might be no refuge from the majority:

> When an individual or a party is wronged in the United States, to whom can he apply for redress? If to public opinion, public opinion constitutes the majority; if to the legislature, it represents the majority and implicitly obeys it; if to the executive power, it is appointed by the majority and serves as a passive tool in its hands. The public force consists of the majority under arms; the jury is the majority invested with the right of hearing judicial cases; and in certain states even the judges are elected by the majority. However iniquitous or absurd the measure of which you complain, you must submit to it as well as you can.

Nonetheless, when the democratic spirit seemed inevitable, conservatism evolved to embrace it by degrees. Arthur Balfour championed a "Tory democracy," explaining that he "saw no point in resisting what was bound to come." Balfour's democracy was still something short of universal suffrage, but it demonstrated the pragmatic direction in which conservative thought was heading. In the end, conservatives reconciled themselves with democracy, but ensured it was implemented with the safeguards necessary to prevent majoritarian tyranny and the erosion of liberty. De Tocqueville argued for a democracy with a judiciary independent of majority sentiment, and a legislature that was representative of the majority without being enslaved by it. Finally, it was another giant of conservatism, the British prime minister Benjamin Disraeli, who extended the franchise to include the working classes.

This underlines a second key concern of conservative thought: the decentralisation of power, or the idea of a mixed, balanced constitution. In the case of British conservatism, that means the sharing of power between the monarchy, the parliament and the commons. The reason for this, obviously, is "that the Prince shall not be able to violate the laws." The words are Burke's, but the sentiments certainly pre-date him, most notably in the writings of Lord Halifax. Moreover, it has remained one of the most influential ideas in Western politics and is the driving force behind our own separation of powers.

"Conservatism is an attitude of mind, not a corpus of doctrine or a carefully worked out system of political theory," wrote Lord Coleraine, Winston Churchill's minister for education. It proceeds from certain insights about human nature, human society and human history, but it is not itself ideological. Indeed, the Burkean suspicion of abstract theories as a basis for government means precisely that conservatism is suspicious of anything ideological. It is not a set of settled political positions or a theory in its own right. It is an *approach* to politics and to social change, what the conservative political philosopher Michael Oakeshott repeatedly called a "disposition." Its chief concern is not with offering a strong vision of the ideal society and a program to achieve it. Accordingly, while conservatism is open to progress, it is not a form of *progressive* politics, which is to say it does not seek to remake the world in pursuit of some ideal or theory. It is therefore not interested in the world of ideological warfare, which is very much a progressive proclivity. Conservatism is occupied instead with the management of the diverse currents and counter-currents that inevitably flow within an organism as complex as human society. Oakeshott explains that the role of conservative government

> is to resolve some of the collisions which this variety of beliefs and
> activities generates; to preserve peace, not by placing an interdict
> upon choice and upon the diversity that springs from the exercise

of preference, not by imposing substantive uniformity, but by enforcing general rules of procedure upon all subjects alike.

Conservatism as articulated by its most seminal interlocutors is inherently broad and pluralistic in a way that progressive, ideological politics so often is not. It may regard with suspicion the handing of power to the uneducated and incompetent working classes, but it does not readily speak of eliminating "enemies of progress." Put another way, conservative political philosophy accepts and even assumes the coexistence of a range of views. Because it does not seek to remake the world in the way revolutionaries do, it does not depend for its survival on unanimity. Implicit here is that conservatism is not troubled by the presence of evil, in the sense that it does not necessarily seek to eliminate it. It recognises that such evil as exists in stable societies, being organic products, cannot simply be removed by force without generating something worse. Conservatism practises what has frequently been called "the politics of imperfection." To return to Oakeshott, the conservative must be prepared to

> rein-in one's own beliefs and desires, to acknowledge the current shape of things, to feel the balance of things in one's hand, to tolerate what is abominable, to distinguish between crime and sin, to respect formality even when it appears to be leading to error …

The end result is a political and philosophical disposition that is not ideologically committed. It is resistant to ideological zeal, but open to the merits of any idea, provided it can be incorporated gradually, organically, with minimum disruption and with respect for traditional forms of life. I will come to consider conservatism's relationship with liberalism soon, but perhaps the fullest expression of what has been discussed so far may be found in the subtle analysis of Lord Hugh Cecil:

> Conservatism is of course in practical politics opposed to Liberalism and to Socialism. But it is not, considered as a system of political thought, directly antagonistic to either. The distinctive characteristic

of Liberalism would perhaps be said to be a regard for liberty. Conservatism is certainly not opposed to liberty. On two sides indeed it inclines towards liberty and defends and upholds it. The liberty of the subject has been so largely the purpose of our constitutional system that no party can champion the traditional Constitution without also defending the principles of liberty ...

If Conservatism be not simply antagonistic to Liberalism, it is clear that in pursuing social reform it must often find itself in sympathy at least with some of the objects of Socialism. But there is in the socialist movement, or at least there appears to Conservative eyes, an element of Jacobinism which is the true antagonist Conservatives have for more than a hundred years opposed. The Jacobin went indeed to lengths to which no reasonable socialist would dream of following, but there is sometimes a taint of Jacobinism in socialist language. We seem sometimes to catch the Jacobin accent of reckless disregard of private rights; of merciless hatred towards those who, perhaps through no fault of their own, have become associated with some real or fancied abuse; of that disposition, not gradually to develop one state of society out of another, but to make a clean sweep of institutions in the interest of a half-thought-out reform ... Conservatism arose to resist Jacobinism, and that is to this day its most essential and fundamental characteristic. But in so far as socialists can be prevailed upon scrupulously to respect the principle of justice and to divest their programme of all traces of vindictiveness, there is nothing to prevent Conservatives considering their proposals, each upon its merits.

Modern conservatism is not comprehensively captured by the conservative tradition outlined above. While it is true that these principles remain conservatism's bedrock, it is impossible to understand modern conservative thought without grasping conservatism's embrace of another tradition in political philosophy: liberalism. Many of the commitments we now call conservative – such as a belief in the free market – proceed directly from liberalism and are not immediately deducible from pre-twentieth-century conservatism. It is often forgotten that the very same French revolutionaries Burke so famously criticised were advocates of the free market. Certainly, some conservatives, like William Lecky, were advocates of capitalism (and opposed democracy on the grounds that it would lead to socialism), but others, like John Ruskin and later Hilaire Belloc, were staunch critics of it. The industrial revolution was, after all, revolutionary in a way that could easily unsettle conservatives. If this now strikes us as an odd thought, it is only because conservatism and liberalism have become so fused in the latter-day political imagination.

Probably the definitive statement of liberalism is John Stuart Mill's classic dissertation *On Liberty*, published in 1859. Mill had grown increasingly concerned about what he perceived to be a growing "liberticide," particularly from those who considered themselves social reformers. Here, he was objecting to the reformers' willingness to sacrifice individual freedom for the sake of society. Mill's blazing contribution was to insist that political structures should do precisely the opposite: protect the individual from the persecution of society. The role of the law and of government is therefore not to impose majority will, but to ensure the liberty of the individual. On this view, society has no right to insist upon conformity. For Mill, the idea that the State has an interest in "the whole bodily and mental discipline of every one of its citizens" and is therefore justified in "the regulation of every part of private conduct" must be resoundingly rejected. In his view, neither society nor the State has any right to interfere with an individual's thought or conduct, unless it is to prevent harm to others. It is from this philosophical starting point that Mill champions freedom of thought and expression, ideals we now take for granted but which were in his time quite radical.

Liberalism's most obvious difference with conservatism is that it has more ideological content: it proposes a positive account of how society should be run. Whereas conservatism most fundamentally stands against something, liberalism is for a stated ideal. It does not necessarily value the status quo unless it is already protective of individual liberty. It believes in the inherent worth of liberty as "the only unfailing and permanent source of improvement." In that sense it is progressive, and it certainly was in Mill's time. Mill was a vocal advocate for women's rights, and in *The Subjugation of Women* he likened the social status of women of his time to that of the slaves, which certainly spoke of progressive aspirations.

Mill assigned very little value to tradition for its own sake. While conservatives were celebrating the collective wisdom embedded in social conventions, Mill's plea for individual liberty proceeded precisely on the basis that people needed protection from the "despotism of custom," which is so often "the standing hindrance to human advancement." People, he argued, should be free to "aim at something better than customary." Accordingly, he valued "different experiments of living." Perhaps unsurprisingly, then, Mill was disdainful of the conservatives of his era. In a letter to a Conservative MP in 1866, he famously declared: "I never meant to say that the Conservatives are generally stupid. I meant to say that stupid people are generally Conservative. I believe that is so obviously and universally admitted a principle that I hardly think any gentleman will deny it."

That said, conservatism and liberalism have significant areas of overlap. In his concern for the plight of the individual Mill has something of an ally in Burke, who (in Lord Hugh Cecil's assessment) "hated and denounced with his whole heart injustice to individuals committed in the course of political or social reform." Mill similarly accused "the majority of moral and social reformers" of resembling "either churches or sects in their assertion of the right of spiritual domination." Mill's project was self-consciously a progressive one intended to improve the human condition, but his rejection of social engineering resonates strongly with the conservative tradition. Like Burke, he recognised the dangers of progressive zeal. "The spirit of improvement is not always a spirit of liberty," he wrote, "for it may aim at forcing improvements on an unwilling people."

Liberalism, while a progressive doctrine, is therefore not progressive in the manner of revolutionary politics. Its approach to social change remains an organic one, which makes it compatible with conservatism in important ways. Liberals may be more philosophically optimistic than conservatives because they have greater faith in the human capacity for improvement, but liberalism and conservatism are united in their opposition to the logic of revolution. Neither accepts the right of a person or a polity to impose radical utopian designs on society, and neither proposes a scheme to rid the world of evil. Both are therefore inherently pluralistic.

The main incongruity between them concerns their attitudes to tradition and custom. Since at least the twentieth century, though, that controversy has been moot. The laws, governance structures and institutions of the West have long since evolved to the point where they embody the principles of liberalism. Freedom of thought and expression are now axiomatic in our society, even if (as in Australia) they do not have much in the way of formal, legal protection (a bill of rights, say). The idea of limited government is so unimpeachable in the United States that almost any comprehensive public service risks being branded socialism. In this modern context, liberalism is fundamentally a conservative political ideology. Its eagerness to defend individual liberty against the intrusions of the State must frustrate the revolutionary project of creating and then forcing compliance with a radically new order. Change in a liberal context occurs through the accumulation of individual action and expression — that is to say, it occurs gradually and through organic processes. Once liberalism itself became institutionally customary and traditional, conservatives had every reason to embrace it.

And they did. Throughout the Western world, and especially in a young nation like Australia that post-dates the aristocratic conservatism against which Mill railed, mainstream conservatism now means *liberal conservatism*. Our urban conservative party is called the *Liberal Party* for that very reason. That party's founder and most revered figure, Robert Menzies, was explicit on the point:

> We took the name Liberal because we were determined to be a progressive party, willing to make experiments, in no sense reactionary, but believing in the individual, his rights and his enterprise, and rejecting the Socialist panacea.

This is why we have come to associate conservatism with a range of ideas anchored in the priority given to individual liberty – including, most famously, a firm belief in free enterprise, low taxation and small government. As the Liberal Party historian Judith Brett has noted, one of the Liberal Party's most strident early criticisms of Labor was that it was collectivist rather than individualist. Labor's were the politics of class, unionism and narrow vested interests; the Liberal Party acted for the entire nation and the individual Australians that constitute it. Labor makes its policies in conferences and demands that its representatives fall in line with the caucus, while the Liberals are a "broad church" of individuals. In crude terms (used particularly during the Menzies era), the Liberal Party charged Labor with being socialist rather than liberal. The language is slightly less dichotomous these days, but the message is similar. Labor are big-spending, centralist, social engineers (socialist); the Liberals are for free enterprise, small business and low spending (liberal). Modern conservatives do not merely derive from Disraeli and Burke. Whatever Mill might have thought of it, they are his children, too. On this, let me cite no less pertinent an authority than John Howard:

> We should never as members of the Liberal Party of Australia lose sight of the fact that we are the trustees of two great political

traditions. We are, of course, the custodian of the classical liberal tradition within our society – Australian Liberals should revere the contribution of John Stuart Mill to political thought. We are also the custodians of the conservative tradition in our community. And if you look at the history of the Liberal Party, it is at its best when it balances and blends those two traditions. Mill and Burke are interwoven into the history and the practice and the experience of our political party.

In light of the above, we can state the fundamental principles of liberal conservatism with relative ease. Because it is conservative, its starting point is that society is a complex organism not susceptible to human comprehension and which has evolved over centuries. For this reason, change should be gradual and organic, not sudden and disruptive. Liberal conservatism does not aspire to the creation of a perfect world, but it is concerned to improve the living conditions of its own population. In keeping with the conservative tradition, a society's enduring institutions should be valued, but power should be shared among them so as to be decentralised, rather than concentrated dangerously in the hands of a small number. This implies the separation of powers, and checks and balances in the system of government.

However, this tradition's inherited liberalism means that State power should also be limited. The State is bound to protect individual rights and freedoms. In particular, it respects freedom of thought and expression, and only intervenes in the lives of its citizens where necessary to prevent harm to another party. By liberal extension, it believes in and facilitates free enterprise (though not necessarily without limitation) and has done so in Australia since Alfred Deakin's Liberal Protectionist Party joined with the Free Trade Party to form Australia's first liberal–conservative coalition in 1909. Importantly, though, that does not necessarily mean the abandonment of the working classes. Australia's dominant liberal tradition stemmed from Deakin, for whom the protection of the working class was of great importance. Deakin established the New Protection, in which working conditions and wages were to be maintained at what he considered a reasonable standard. Similarly in the conservative tradition, Disraeli was deeply concerned with the "condition of the multitude [and] with a desire to improve and elevate it." Notably, that meant conservatives had to "effect some reduction of their hours of labour and humanise their toil." Accordingly, Disraeli introduced legislation in favour of trade unions. As Lord Hugh Cecil argued, conservatism is

> unwilling to acquiesce in the sufferings of the people from poverty and its attendant evils. Hence Conservatism comes also to be identified with measures of social improvement designed to raise the condition of the poor.

Seen through liberal conservative eyes, the citizenry is a collection of individuals, not of groups. Certainly, citizens have the freedom to form social groups and take on collective identities as they wish, but these groupings are not the basis for people's treatment by the State. Some old institutional groups might have a legislative position – most notably trade unions – but in general, the citizen's rights, freedoms and obligations flow from her or his existence as an individual and not from any group affiliation. This partly explains the lengthy tradition in conservative Australian politics of attacking Labor as the party of sectionalism: of class in the first instance, and more recently of minorities and special-interest groups. Groupism, on this view, divides the nation and also compromises liberty because it limits an individual's autonomy. It binds the individual to the ideals and fate of others, thereby restricting the potential for "experiments of living," the capacity to imagine and pursue one's own destiny.

In Australia, this has very much informed the liberal conservative approach to indigenous affairs, particularly once Aborigines were granted full citizenship in 1967. Were they a distinct group in society, bonded by a shared and deeply traumatic history, or were they citizens of the nation, indistinguishable from other Australians in the eyes of the State? This, of course, was scarcely a problem that confronted Mill in nineteenth-century England. Australia's circumstances, though, were emphatically different. And while there is a perfectly respectable conservative argument for recognising this group identity on the basis that it is an organic phenomenon, inseparable from the circumstances of history, the conservative marriage with liberalism has meant such recognition is hardly instinctive. The difference may be philosophical, but the implications are very much practical. ATSIC, native title, any kind of treaty and indeed almost the entire politics of symbolic reconciliation are very difficult to accommodate in a liberal conservative worldview. Each requires the recognition of Aborigines as a distinct group within the citizenry. How, for instance, can a nation have a treaty with its own citizens? How can it recognise a form of title that, as a matter of law, is open only to some citizens and not all?

One should be circumspect, then, about explaining every liberal conservative position on these issues as the simple product of racism or colonialism. These factors may be present in varying degrees, but there is a strong philosophical dimension that is fundamental. Recall that the liberal conservative believes that group recognition is a barrier to freedom; in the extreme, it is a form of oppression. To accept the group-based progressive approach to indigenous affairs is, in John Howard's words, to render Aborigines "permanently … as citizens apart, unable to participate in the mainstream of Australian life, even where they wished to do so."

The foundational values outlined above, it should be noted, are overwhelmingly *institutional* rather than personal. Liberal conservatism promotes and defends ideals such as individual freedom, the rule of law, the integrity of parliament and the separation of powers. It is not ideologically concerned with the personal attitudes and values of the citizenry because both its conservatism and its commitment to individual liberty hold that the State has no legitimate role in determining them. The beliefs and values of society are matters of organic development, not government declaration. Here, for instance, is John Howard in his 1997 Australia Day speech:

The beliefs that we have about what it is to be an Australian are not things that can be imposed from above by political leaders of any persuasion. They are not things that can be generated by [a] self-appointed cultural elite who seek to tell us what our identity ought to be … our identity … is never something that can be imposed.

Howard, at this time a newly elected prime minister, was attacking his predecessor, Paul Keating, who had so aggressively promoted a progressive cultural agenda based around reconciliation, republicanism and Australia's integration with Asia. Howard rejected Keating's position on all these matters, but his point here is more general. In principle, it does not matter what values and identity are being promoted. The point is that it is not the government's place to dictate them. In accordance with the liberal conservative tradition, politicians – "of any persuasion" – should not be lecturing citizens on what they should value or believe.

Nothing in the above account should be taken to imply that liberal conservatism dogmatically eschews government intervention in the economy. Indeed, for the overwhelming majority of conservatives and even liberals, some level of government activity was a given. While Mill does not deal extensively with the issue in *On Liberty*, he does say that governments "cannot have too much of the kind of activity which does not impede, but aids and stimulates, individual exertion and development." Mill also went on to support the idea of income redistribution programs in favour of the poor. We have already seen how key figures, like Disraeli, accepted government's responsibility to act to preserve a minimum level of welfare for its people, as did Winston Churchill. In Australia, Robert Menzies accepted that "there are many activities … which cannot be left and have not been left to private enterprise," particularly in "a young and vast country." For Menzies, government enterprises are often "a foundation upon which the efforts of private entrepreneurs can build." As John Hirst has noted, Australia has tended to have an activist government, born of the fact that it was a new country that needed to be built from the ground up. Our rulers, unlike their British counterparts, "built roads and bridges, improved ports, encouraged exploration, surveyed land for settlement, and provided settlers with their labour force."

This reflects the liberal orthodoxy that prevailed after World War II. The economy would be powered by free, private enterprise, but government intervention was thought necessary to provide certain public services, overcome the effects of market failure and ensure a minimum standard of living for citizens. Thus emerged the welfare state. This economic model, often called a "mixed economy," found differing expressions throughout the world. In Scandinavia, for instance, governments provided extensive services and benefits funded by high taxes. The British model imposed lower taxes and featured less government involvement, and focused on providing services, such as transport, energy and health, that were either essential or not sufficiently profitable for private enterprise. In parts of continental Europe, government intervention focused on benefits, not services. In each case, though, the central idea was that the government acted as a bulwark against the market's potential ravages.

This approach, most famously championed by the liberal economist John Maynard Keynes, was very much a product of its time. Keynes had witnessed the Great Depression and then the horror of World War II. The two events may easily be linked. Fascist politics of the kind that emerged in Nazi Germany is very often the consequence of national trauma. Nazism rose to popularity after the Depression, when the emasculated middle class leapt sharply to ultra-nationalism and blamed the Jews for their plight. The pattern was repeated elsewhere, too. Latin America, which was hit particularly savagely because of its significant trade links with the United States, retreated into a shrill form of nationalism, ushering in the rise of fascism across the continent. The Netherlands witnessed a series of riots, increased xenophobia and the emergence of the National Socialist Party.

These are the kinds of connections Keynes made. After World War I, he published *The Economic Consequences of the Peace*, in which he argued passionately for Germany's war debts to France, Britain and the United States to be written down. When these nations insisted on high reparations, Keynes foresaw the crippling of Germany and the rise of German anger, then vengeance. And that is basically what transpired. The Depression was particularly devastating for Germany precisely because so much of the national economy was financed by American loans. When the New York share market collapsed, there was nothing to mitigate the disaster.

It is therefore easy to understand how Keynes came to value economic and social stability. Keynes looked at World War II and saw a nation that veered towards fascism as a result of insecurity, anger and humiliation. Hence he argued that government involvement in the economy, which would still ultimately be powered by the free market, would introduce stability both to the economy and to society. Government enterprise could stimulate a flagging economy, and be stripped back in boom times to stop the economy overheating. Meanwhile the welfare state would provide people with economic security, thereby minimising the likelihood of social disruption. The welfare state became popular after the war partly because Keynes' predictions had come true and partly as a way of minimising the appeal of communism, which was growing as an international political force. Keynes' economic idea was radical, but it was influenced by a deeply conservative imperative: stability, not just in an economic but a social sense.

Keynes, however, was far from the only liberal economist drawing post-war conclusions. Friedrich Hayek left his native Austria in the inter-war period. During this time, the country experienced a socialist government, a coup, and then finally annexation to the German Third Reich. It was a spectacularly swift transition from liberalism to Nazism, for which Hayek blamed Austria's socialist experimentation. The failure of the centrally planned economy had opened the door to malevolent, reactionary forces. The solution, then, was to keep government as distant as possible from economic activity. Hayek saw the Keynesian trend not merely as bad economics, but as a precursor to the destruction of liberty and the emergence of tyranny. It was, as he titled his classic 1944 work, *The Road to Serfdom*. Hayek's was an anti-collectivist argument of the most emphatic sort.

Hayek is often credited with fathering the phenomenon we now call "neo-liberalism," and which Kevin Rudd derisively dubs "market fundamentalism." Hayek did sometimes describe himself and his colleagues as neo-liberal, but that fact alone is misleading if one assumes this means he believed in the market being left entirely to itself. In fact, these economists used the term "neo-liberal" precisely as a way of *distancing* themselves from pure *laissez-faire* economics. The original neo-liberals, including Hayek, were not concerned merely with State involvement, but first and foremost with concentrations of *power* – any power. That included the power of private actors, as the German neo-liberal Walter Eucken observed: "The grant of freedom can become a threat to freedom if it allows the formation of private power."

Eucken also noted that "like all of history, economic history is replete with abuses of power." His neo-liberalism rejected pure *laissez-faire* economics on precisely the basis that the market left to its own devices would advantage the most powerful entities and could consolidate monopolies. Powerful corporations could use their overwhelming market share to destroy their competitors and then become a coercive force. Additionally, this would confer political power upon them so that what looked like State interventions in the public interest were in fact interventions taken at the behest of powerful economic actors.

All such concentrations of economic power – trusts, cartels, even unions – were therefore threats to liberty in much the same way as excessive government intervention would be. Accordingly, the first neo-liberals did not believe the State should vanish. On the contrary they advocated a State strong enough to fight and even dismantle monopolies, to ensure competition and to provide conditions conducive to the market's proper operation. The State should ensure proper information flow so that market actors were acting in the best possible knowledge. It should enforce contracts, implement commercial law and protect property rights. Hayek even argued that the State could legitimately regulate hours of work. The fatal flaw in *laissez-faire* capitalism was that it placed in the hands of the market not only the *conduct* of economic activity, but also the *framework* in which it was conducted. Neo-liberalism asked for a State that vacated the former, but maintained the latter.

So far, so liberal. But so conservative? The suspicion of centralised power has some conservative appeal and Churchill seems to have been initially impressed with Hayek's ideas. He campaigned on a non-Keynesian platform for the 1945 election, but lost heavily on polling day and the Tories quickly identified themselves with Keynes. In their 1950 policy document, they boasted of their role in passing government-provided social services in Britain. They also claimed credit for designing the principles on which pensions, sickness and unemployment benefits, the industrial injustices benefit and the national health scheme were based.

Such thinking was so at odds with Hayek's that he saw it necessary to strike back in an essay called *Why I Am Not a Conservative*, explaining why he rejected "any conservatism which deserves to be called such." Hayek's objection was an old one: conservatism is about caution and resistance to change, but does not propose anything of itself: "by its very nature it cannot offer an alternative to the direction in which we are moving." Conservatives praise growth and progress, but only in the past. In the present they are opposed to it. The liberal, by contrast, embraces any change that enhances individual liberty, even without knowing precisely what its consequences will be.

Hayek understood that conservatism's marriage with liberalism was an artefact of history, not a philosophical necessity. Before socialism arrived, liberalism and conservatism were sworn enemies. After World War II, however, the Keynesian consensus had driven conservatism back towards socialism, evident in the "Middle Way" policies of Conservative British prime minister Harold Macmillan. Conservatives were inherently fond of authority and suspicious of uncontrolled social processes. They therefore could not bring themselves to submit the development of society to the untamed, unpredictable logic of the market. Keynesian economics, with its balance of government and market power, appealed to their sense of order. It could not accept a State that was there merely to sustain the market. In a stroke, Hayek had revived the dormant contradictions between liberalism and conservatism by articulating a more extreme version of liberalism than the mainstream.

Hayek's assessment of conservatism was, in my view, partially inaccurate. For him, conservatism was hostile to individual liberty and dangerously fond of strong authority. This characterisation overlooks the longstanding conservative advocacy of decentralised power. It also does not account for the fact that the preservation of liberty had been one of the reasons conservatives were reluctant to hand political power to the working classes. Hayek even begins from a position with which conservatism is deeply sympathetic: that human knowledge is too limited to grasp the complexity of social affairs. Human societies are the product of an evolutionary process, and their most enduring institutions are therefore a part of that evolution, rather than the product of deliberate design. Society is a spontaneous order rather than a constructed one, and because of the limits of human knowledge, any interference with it as a way of improving it may end up being counter-productive. It is therefore far better to allow individuals to pursue their own ends through their own initiatives. Civilisation, in Hayek's view, is the product of innumerable social accidents, some of which we choose to keep. The parallels with the idea of the market are obvious.

But these qualifications aside, Hayek is quite correct to identify a gulf between conservatism and his neo-liberalism. To appreciate this we must first understand that neo-liberalism is not truly an economic theory; it is a political ideology. Its economic program stems from its political concerns, not the reverse. Neo-liberalism is above all a prescription for freedom. Government interference in the economy is an evil because it is the road to serfdom, not merely because it hampers economic growth.

The radicalism in this idea is not simply that it is political — Keynesian economics is, too. Neo-liberalism, however, conceives of society in a profoundly radical way. It sees life, and therefore society, entirely through the lens of the market. The market therefore becomes far more than an economic concept: it becomes an organising principle for politics and for society. This transforms the market from a phenomenon into a philosophy. The implications are profound. Everything becomes, in principle, subject to a market calculus. Concepts such as justice and morality, for instance, become whatever the market says they are. It is not for the State (or anyone else) to determine justice, for that becomes an expression of arbitrary State power. The State should merely administer contracts and enforce laws that sustain the market.

For this reason, Hayek despised the idea of "social justice" — and its associated concerns for equality and fairness — which he considered an artifice devoid of meaning. As he argued in The Mirage of Social Justice, it is pointless to evaluate the market's operations through the prism of justice. "To speak of justice," he insisted, "always implies that some person or persons ought, or ought not, to have performed some action." But since market consequences are spontaneous rather than planned, they are not the result of any person's conduct and are therefore neither just nor unjust. Certainly, the market's distribution of burdens and benefits "would in many instances have to be regarded as very unjust if it were the result of a deliberate allocation to particular people." But since it is not, these consequences are to be accepted, rather than modified or regulated. The fact that the market produces a result is sufficient to make it proper even if some think it unfair, provided that the market is free and competitive. Neo-liberalism therefore precipitates what we might call a "market society." It is here that neo-liberalism begins to distinguish itself from its more mainstream ancestors.

Markets, of course, are amoral. They do not function on the basis of external moral considerations. They have only one necessary value: efficiency. A market society, therefore, is not concerned with what is "right," for that is arbitrary. It is concerned only with what is efficient. This is a radically different basis for social action than that which any society has known previously. As neo-liberal thought spread around the world and evolved, the use of market rationality (particularly in America) began to find its logical consequences. At an extreme, neo-liberal thinkers used economic concepts to determine appropriate government policies on crime and punishment, as the Chicago School's Gary Becker did so successfully. Theft, for instance, is criminal because it forcibly redistributes wealth but does not create it. Thieves spend time planning and executing their crimes, but that time is unproductive. Meanwhile, potential victims waste resources on unproductive security measures. In the final analysis, then, theft is a problem not principally because it violates anything that is inherently sacred. It is a problem because it is unproductive and inefficient. Similarly, fines are a superior form of punishment to imprisonment because they are more efficient. Fining offenders gives the State revenue. Imprisoning them is costly. It is also less of a deterrent (at least in Becker's analysis).

And, of course, there is no reason to stop at crime. Applying the logic of the market, each social interaction becomes a competitive event. Each individual citizen becomes an entrepreneur, and each social action becomes an investment. Citizens in the market state do not seek education to better themselves or for its inherent value. They seek it to make themselves a more valuable commodity. That suggests another radical social consequence: in a market society, things obtain value only once they are commodified, because they do not have an inherent cultural or ethical value, as tradition might have had it. This in turn encourages the commodification of everything as a basis for social interaction. Nothing, not even religion or sex, is beyond this commodification process. Similarly, because the social world becomes in principle indistinguishable from the economic world, social problems invite market-based solutions. For every problem we become inclined to search for a product: self-help CDs, endless pharmaceuticals, miracle cures. In this way, neo-liberalism ultimately remakes culture in the market's image. It generates a public discourse anchored in market terminology. People are labour. Politicians have political capital. When Becker first proposed the concept of human capital, the idea was widely considered repugnant. No longer.

Within this framework, it makes no sense to ask what should be done about the market's negative consequences. By definition, there are none. Everything from heightened inequality to environmental degradation is to be tolerated in a neo-liberal world because neo-liberalism lacks any vigorous means of critiquing its own consequences. In this way it is a closed ideological system.

Neo-liberalism is *neo* for a reason: it is derivative from liberalism but importantly distinct. And at this point it is possible to identify where neo-liberalism parts ways from its classical forebear. It begins with the same basic premises: a fundamental concern for individual liberty, a corresponding advocacy of a free market and a desire for a small, non-coercive State. These are important continuities. But the differences begin with the neo-liberal conception of society as something constituted through the market. The "only ties which hold the whole of a Great Society together are purely 'economic,'" wrote Hayek. By this, he meant that society is the product of people pursuing their own diverse ends, through common means. It is not based on any shared understanding of what those ends should be. By implication, society is not ultimately based on any sense of shared values or culture, but on a shared means by which people may pursue their "individuality."

In this sense, society is spontaneous and evolutionary. But this brings with it a sense that any other concept of society is artificial. Neo-liberalism easily collapses into a theory of pure individualism that risks doing away with society altogether. "There is no such thing as society," declared Margaret Thatcher during her avowedly (though not perfectly) neo-liberal premiership. Thatcher was making the point that it was not for the State to solve people's problems, such as homelessness. The market is not a forum for shared destinies and obligations to fellow citizens, and neither, primarily, is the market society.

Mill understood that liberal societies were bound together by an understanding of the cultures that produced them. That is to say, Mill understood that societies were held together by a glue that does not necessarily obey market rationality. In his *Principles of Political Economy* he described as "essentially repulsive" a society "only held together by the relations and feelings arising out of pecuniary interests." That is very much consistent with conservative notions of society as arising from shared histories, cultures and customs. There is something more "real" to the traditional liberal and conservative concepts of society; something that is more than merely manufactured by market interactions. The same is true of the concept of the individual self. As we have seen, the neo-liberal individual is a market-based actor, both entrepreneur and consumer. There is not a great deal more content to this individual. He or she does not appear to have particularly strong connections to history, culture and the identities they forge. The neo-liberal individual is a kind of *Homo economicus*.

Liberalism maintains that market outcomes have their own wisdom. For this reason, like neo-liberalism, it does not regard equality as a desirable goal, and it is quite comfortable with unequal income distributions. But neo-liberalism's transformation of the market into a political rationality takes this stance quite radically further, even if unintentionally. Liberalism seeks a free market, neo-liberalism posits a world in which there is very little outside the market. The comprehensive commodification of life extends the market well beyond its traditional territory of goods and services. The market, therefore, need not trade in anything "real." Put another way, if nothing is valuable in neo-liberal terms unless the market assigns it a value, then the reverse must also be true: anything to which the market assigns a value is axiomatically valuable. The logic of neo-liberalism (but not of Mill's liberalism) is that new transactions are invented for old services. A series of short-term labour contracts, for instance, is more desirable than permanent employment because it is more flexible, and therefore more responsive to and consonant with market forces. This is the philosophical engine behind the explosive growth of the finance industry. The creation of ever more complex and artificial financial products in many cases does not create anything new, but it generates a flurry of market activity, which in neo-liberal terms is some kind of advance. Since the global financial crisis gripped the public imagination, the emptiness of much of the finance industry has become something of a symbol of neo-liberalism's failures. More accurately, though, it is an expression of its essence.

Almost nothing about this is conservative. In fact, neo-liberalism's radically market-based view of the social world is deeply un-conservative in several important ways. By viewing the market as a philosophy, it accepts that the market must be maintained, and even created, through the use of State power, as a means of safeguarding liberty. The market may be an example of a spontaneous order, but in neo-liberal hands it is also a desirable social structure, whether or not it is naturally occurring. If necessary, it must be made. This is precisely, as Hayek would urge, a thoroughly progressive ideology. Neo-liberalism is unashamedly a means of reconstructing the social world, and in that sense a quasi-utopian project. It may not seek to create the perfect world, but it does seek to create a world of perfect individual liberty, which it holds as the ultimate goal of politics. This thoroughly ideological design is not the way that conservatives have traditionally approached the human condition. Neo-liberalism is, after all, the theoretical product of philosophers. That is precisely what conservatism rejects as a legitimate means of social change.

Many un-conservative results flow from this. By its nature, neo-liberalism embraces risk and the unknown; conservatism is cautious and risk-averse. Neo-liberalism respects only those social institutions that are compatible with the market; conservatism cherishes established institutions for their own sake, and for the stability and continuity they provide. Neo-liberalism is, therefore, quite prepared to sweep away cultural norms and social structures that cannot be rationalised in market terms, quite inconsistently with the conservative reverence for the mysterious qualities of society and the desire for gradual change that is organic rather than ardently ideological in origin. Neo-liberalism regards judgments about the quality of people's living and working conditions as arbitrary; conservatism has a tradition of seeking refinement in people's living and working lives, based on non-market ideas of what is desirable. Neo-liberalism promotes its political program as a universal truth; conservatism is suspicious of such claims and is attentive to the limitations imposed by local circumstances.

The last point deserves elaboration. Because neo-liberalism regards any other political arrangement as vulnerable to tyranny, it conceives of itself as a program for the world. It is therefore paradigmatically globalist; in Hayek's phrase, it "respect[s] no boundaries," while conservatism is designed to value them as established institutional features. In a worldview where politics is subordinated to the logic of the market, conventional political borders are, like so much political action, arbitrary. The ideal neo-liberal market is therefore a boundless one that for Hayek "tends to make mankind One World." The global economy is one such world, and, accordingly, barriers to trade within that market are an intolerable State intervention. The aim is not merely to create a market society, but to create a global one.

The logical extension of this is nothing less than the comprehensive recasting of world politics. The concept of national sovereignty must necessarily be compromised to facilitate a global free market. Since people are units of labour, their movement should be as unhindered as the market itself. A neo-liberal world is therefore a world of free immigration, because immigration restrictions become a form of protectionism. It has no room for localism and certainly not for parochialism. The world must be integrated into a unit. The cultural and institutional differences that prevail across the globe are of only peripheral importance here, waiting for the power of the market to overcome them and generate a new global market culture.

In an era of nation-states, that creates an irreconcilable contradiction between political structure and political reality. A globalised, integrated world, built on the back of a globalised economy (even if not perfectly realised), is one where cause and effect are not necessarily limited by geography. And yet the nation-state is a resolutely geographical concept. To see this contradiction in action, we need only look as far as the present financial crisis, which originated in America and quickly bankrupted Iceland. As the stock market crashed in late 2008, the entire world was fixated on a bail-out package being considered by the United States Congress that many hoped would limit the damage. These were not politicians we elected. We are not connected to them through an authoritative political structure. And yet their impact on our lives was, at least at that moment, greater than that of almost every politician we do elect. Ours is now a world of global consequences and national politics, which is, of course, profoundly and structurally undemocratic. That sort of structural contradiction is precisely what conservative political philosophy is designed to avoid. Its emphasis on gradual, organic change means that political structures should be given time to evolve in step with social and economic change. Where neo-liberalism implies the creation of a single global market culture, conservatism intuits the dangerous impossibility of such a project.

"The main significance of Hayek's *The Road to Serfdom*," wrote Michael Oakeshott, is "not the cogency of his doctrine, but the fact that it is a doctrine. A plan to resist all planning may be better than its opposite, but it belongs to the same style of politics." In the final analysis, this must be the most fundamental conservative objection to neo-liberalism. Any conservatism that embraces it is necessarily a conservatism transformed, perhaps unrecognisably.

THE COMING OF NEO-LIBERALISM

Much of the above is a theoretical account of neo-liberalism's social and political dimensions. For that reason it is artificially absolute. Like any ideology, neo-liberalism can never operate so purely in practice, and never did. Nevertheless, much of the above sounds anything but foreign. The social implications of neo-liberal theory have become familiar points of public debate. The concept of consumer culture, for instance, scarcely needs elaboration because it has become embedded in our reality. The point, though, for the purposes of this essay, is not the degree to which neo-liberal economics has been implemented; it is the fact that its underlying vision of society has been absorbed. This is a process that began thirty years ago.

In some ways it is odd that it did. Hayek's dire predictions for a Keynesian world were never fulfilled. In spite of its national health service and its welfare state, Britain never descended into totalitarianism. Nor did Sweden, with its high taxes and government involvement in the economy. Keynesianism, though, ran into considerable problems of its own. Keynes had held that inflation and unemployment were polar opposites to be managed by government action. The model fell apart in the mid-1970s when Western economies (especially Britain's) were struck with both high inflation and high unemployment, along with low growth. After thirty glorious years, Keynesianism's political dominance was at an end.

With the consensus unravelling, politicians were seeking new ideas, and neo-liberalism emerged to fill the breach. Hayek was in from the cold, and neo-liberalism became the dominant political ideology in Western politics for the next three decades. That of itself is not remarkable: politics is a series of turning points, full of ideological triumphs, demises and resurrections. But of interest here is that the neo-liberal pioneers who so radically transformed the Western political landscape were not self-described political progressives. At least in party-political terms, they were conservatives. In Britain, the key turning point was the election in 1979 of Margaret Thatcher, who immediately embarked on a program of neo-liberal reform. She placed a limit on government spending, cut funding to education and housing, privatised an enormous number of government enterprises, lowered direct income taxes and crushed the trade unions (which Hayek despised). Thatcher was a very public devotee of Hayek. She had met him as opposition leader and feted him as prime minister. She appointed Hayekian thinkers to her ministry. She also had a trans-Atlantic ally in Ronald Reagan, who famously declared in his inauguration speech that "Government is not the solution to our problems; government is the problem." Reagan, too, introduced sweeping tax cuts and reduced government spending on health, education and environmental protection.

These reforms were controversial, especially in Britain, where Thatcher battled awful approval ratings and dissent within her party as well as rising unemployment. It is from this period that we derive the political descriptors "wet" and "dry" in conservative party politics. The "dries" sided with Thatcher's neo-liberal reform agenda. The "wets" were more sceptical, believing that the State still had a social and economic role to play beyond being a mere market facilitator. One famous story recounted in John Ranelagh's *Thatcher's People* has the Iron Lady shouting down a "Middle Way" colleague by holding up a copy of Hayek's *The Constitution of Liberty* and declaring, "This is what we believe." At the time Thatcher was a newly appointed opposition leader, but the ideological division continued into her first term as prime minister, particularly when unemployment was at its worst. Those divisions eventually became a thing of the past and neo-liberalism assumed the status of conventional wisdom. That transition is explained by several factors, among them the economic recovery that finally arrived in Britain. But to understand neo-liberalism's impressive dominance as a political ideology, it is necessary to place it in the context of international politics, and especially the Cold War.

The Cold War was a perfectly distilled contest of ideologies: communism against capitalism; state-run economies against the free market; big government against small government; labour against capital. In the geo-politics of the Cold War, the entire world was so bifurcated. Every nation was deemed either an ally of the Soviet Union or the United States. At stake was sole superpower status and the power to remake the world order along the victor's ideological lines. The liberal/communist divide had attained an almost impossible urgency. Never had it been so alive, so intense, so potentially cataclysmic.

Inevitably, this had a significant impact on domestic politics. It is not that the ideological divide was new: twentieth-century party politics often centred on the contest between labour and capital, between collectivism and entrepreneurs, between society and the individual. Indeed, these divisions have been encoded in our political script ever since liberalism and conservatism combined: party politics in Australia, New Zealand, Ireland and Britain is a contest between a labour party and a conservative party. But the Cold War took these divisions to an ideological extreme, turning one side of the argument into something beyond the pale, some-thing sympathetic to the great external threat of the age. As already noted, the Menzies-era Coalition often played to the theme of a socialist Labor Party. In short, the discourse of domestic politics, like international relations, became ideologically charged in a way that was new.

That did not automatically mean neo-liberalism was in vogue. Indeed, for most (if not all) of the Cold War, it wasn't. But the polarised world certainly prepared the ground for neo-liberalism's emergence. Soviet communism was an extreme form of collectivist, progressive politics; neo-liberalism is its ideological opposite: a radical form of liberal, market-driven politics.

Thatcher and Reagan were quintessential Cold Warriors. During the 1970s, Western powers had adopted a policy of *détente* which aimed to ease tensions with the Soviet Union. This began to change when the Soviets invaded Afghanistan in 1979, when Western powers started moving towards a politics of deterrence. Reagan's election in 1980 marked an acceleration of this approach. He quickly escalated the conflict, spending large amounts on building up the US military. His America was a producer of bombers and missiles. The arms race was on in earnest. Reagan provided aid to anti-communist forces throughout the world, fighting the Soviet Union indirectly through a series of "proxy wars." The most (in)famous of these was his support for the Mujahideen in Afghanistan – the very band of fighters that would splinter and evolve into Al-Qa'ida in the coming decades. Thatcher, meanwhile, lent Reagan her unwavering support. She allowed the United States to station cruise missiles in England and supported the deployment of American missiles elsewhere in Europe. At home, she also increased government spending on defence as part of the deterrence policy.

All this complemented their deeply ideological view of the Cold War. *Détente* had reflected a geo-strategic approach whereby ideological differences would be managed. It was the preferred approach of the Republican president Richard Nixon (and his adviser Henry Kissinger). Neither Thatcher nor Reagan was sympathetic to that worldview. It was the Soviets who dubbed Thatcher the "Iron Lady" while she was opposition leader, after she declared the Soviet Union a malevolent empire, driven by violence and an unquenchable thirst for world domination. Reagan took the opportunity of an address before both houses of the British parliament in 1982 to vow to leave "Marxism-Leninism on the ash-heap of history." For them, communism simply had to be vanquished.

This was a world of black and white, of right and wrong, of good and evil. That is to say, it was a paradigmatically *progressive* world, at odds with conservatism's many shades of grey. As a political philosophy, conservatism is not at home in such an ardently ideological atmosphere. (This, in part, was Hayek's objection to it.) As we have seen, conservatism is more an approach to social change than an ideology in its own right. Indeed, it is naturally suspicious of all ideologies. But war, of whatever temperature, has its own kind of osmosis, whereby sworn enemies begin to resemble one another in ways they don't always perceive. In that way, the ideological passions of the Cold War took conservatives with them.

A local example from back in the 1950s may serve to illustrate this tendency. In Australia, the Menzies government passed a bill banning the Communist Party. It was a radical piece of legislation that gave the parliament the power to declare any individual or group to be communist and therefore illegal. This was an extraordinary thing for a liberal conservative leader to do: inconsistent with liberalism's tolerance for freedom of conscience and assembly, conferring arbitrary power upon the executive, and contemptuous of Australia's liberal institutions. And that is what the High Court found when it ultimately ruled that the law was unconstitutional. No doubt Menzies was motivated partly by political strategy: he was searching for a double-dissolution trigger and thought (incorrectly) that the Labor Party might give it to him by defeating the bill in the Senate. But it is also clear that Menzies had an ideological drive here. In the following year he took the nation to a failed referendum that would have given the Commonwealth power to make laws with respect to communists and communism, and would have cleared the way for fresh legislation banning the Communist Party. Communism, being a staunchly ideological foe, produced a similarly ideological response from Western powers. Conservatism's instinctive preference for stability, caution and calm was helplessly overcome by the prevailing political currents. That did not make it neo-liberal immediately, but it rendered it more sympathetic to such un-conservative patterns of political thought.

The official end of the Cold War in 1989 was a momentous event in ideological politics. Like its Eastern European communist allies, the Soviet Union had descended into economic ruin, and was forced to concede to the United States. The Cold War was largely an ideological argument, and with communism's ignominious collapse, the argument had been won. Neo-liberalism already held the reins in Britain and the United States. Now it could do so as world champion; henceforth it would be without any serious challenge internationally as the basis for political organisation. Francis Fukuyama famously scribbled that the Cold War did not signal merely the failure of communism or a new phase in international politics, but "the end of history" itself – a position no conservative could possibly believe, but which was a progressivist's dream. All arguments had now been concluded: humanity had discovered the ultimate, unimpeachable political program. Enter the triumphant "Washington Consensus," which quite closely approximates neo-liberal economics and came to be its real-world expression. This doctrine held that governments should deregulate their economies, liberalise trade and privatise state enterprises – such as health, communications and transport – as much as possible. The Soviets had proven that government could be relied upon to deliver nothing. This was not a uniquely Soviet lesson; it was an abstract, absolute truth to be accepted and implemented globally.

The political centre of gravity had shifted seismically. Conservative parties may have been the first to embrace neo-liberal ideas, but this did not mean such parties were guaranteed government, or that labour parties were excluded from power. Far from it: in Australia, Labor ruled for thirteen years, from the last stages of the Cold War into its aftermath. Rather, it meant something more profound: that parties with more collectivist political traditions reinvented themselves in line with the new neo-liberal consensus. Politics became a contest between shades of a broadly similar ideology. Witness how, after eighteen years of opposition beginning with Thatcher's victory, the British Labour Party repackaged itself under Tony Blair as New Labour. And new it was. Gone was the party of the working class, trade unions and government intervention. Blair's Labour was a pro-market party courting aspirational middle Britons on the basis of their potential as individual entrepreneurs. London became the preferred destination of the world's super-rich and multi-national corporations, and Britain rode the wave of a booming financial sector. Despite revelations that the wealthiest companies are massive tax evaders, New Labour has failed to close the legal loopholes that make this possible, probably for fear of being branded anti-business. Such radical transformations were inevitable. After all, what did it mean to be a labour party in a world where the ideological debate had been resolved in favour of capital? Blair preached a post-ideological "Third Way" in much the same way as the post-war Keynesian conservatives preached a "Middle Way."

The Hawke and Keating governments are similarly illustrative. They shrugged off the imperatives of union politics to reduce tariffs and float the dollar, thereby exposing Australia to the global economy. They abandoned central wage-fixing and moved towards enterprise bargaining between employers and employees, which took them further away from their traditional terrain of siding unremittingly with labour against capital. The trouble for Australian conservatives was that they witnessed this transformation from opposition. With the Labor Party suddenly assuming the role of deregulator and pushing Australia into the global marketplace, the Coalition had to decide whether or not to sign up to the reform agenda. It is at this point that it experienced the same internal division between "wets" and "dries" that Thatcher's Tories had in the previous decade.

The wet/dry division in the Liberal Party was driven locally by the emergence of an informal lobbying force popularly known as the New Right. Their method was to push aggressively for labour-market deregulation in public discourse, but also in court. Among them were experienced barristers, such as Peter Costello, who ran large-scale industrial relations cases against unions, some of which were enormously significant and enormously successful. Chris Puplick, a "wet" Liberal, told the prominent political journalist Paul Kelly that

> New Right ideas gained a high degree of acceptance within the Liberal Party because the Thatcher and Reagan models appeared to be working. The stories you read were about the US economy booming and everything coming up roses in London. When people went to the United Kingdom, they went to London, not Glasgow, Liverpool or Merseyside, to see the human cost of Thatcherism. Everybody went to New York but nobody went north of Central Park or saw what was happening in the American cities under Reagan.

The conflict was a protracted and bitter one. A series of leaks from within the Liberals revealed a party holding meetings with major business stakeholders only to collapse into vehement and embarrassing disagreement over policy. The result was a parade of short-lived leaderships: Andrew Peacock (twice), John Howard, John Hewson and Alexander Downer. The matter was only finally resolved when John Howard won the Liberal Party leadership for the second time and proceeded to defeat Keating in the 1996 election. The Liberal Party is very much a party defined by its leader, and Howard was very "dry" indeed. In fact, he had given the New Right great momentum during his first leadership when he fought off ideological foes within the Liberal Party to establish a new, dry industrial-relations policy. The New Right had moved from the margins of political discourse in the mid-1980s to the centre of the Liberal Party in a few short years. As George Brandis recalled later:

> The most important thing that happened in the Liberal Party in the 1980s, and the current prime minister [John Howard] deserves much credit for pioneering this debate, was encouraging the Liberal Party to abandon that part of the Deakinite tradition which represented economic conservatism and protectionism and to embrace market liberalism.

In Australia, Howard was described as an economic rationalist. In the terms used in this essay, his economic convictions were very much inspired by neo-liberalism. Indeed, Howard's main criticism of Labor was that it had not gone far enough, particularly on industrial-relations reform. For today's Australia this is, of course, an infamous theme, which culminated in Howard's WorkChoices policy. Here was about as pure a distillation of neo-liberalism as politics is likely to provide. Its underlying philosophy treated workers as little more than units of labour, no different from any other commodity to which the market would assign a price. The argument used consistently by Howard and his employment ministers was that lower wages necessarily meant lower unemployment, echoing the neo-liberal belief that high wages represent the only genuine obstacle to full employment. Put simply, if the cost of labour falls enough, everyone will have a job. That means giving employers the power to reduce wages and costly working conditions such as paid leave and overtime. Keynes, by contrast, had held that wages were "sticky": there is a level of payment below which workers will simply refuse to work. Of course, the tale of the 2007 election is one of labour reasserting its value beyond that of a mere commodity. The voters wanted security and good working conditions, and were simply not interested in arguments about how they might reduce unemployment by sacrificing these. They preferred to stick with their own lived experience than to submit to an ideological promise. The electorate, in other words, was conservative.

WorkChoices was anything but an electoral calculation. There was no popular thirst for such radical workplace reform, and it is highly unlikely Howard saw it as a populist move. Rather, it was a nakedly ideological project, facilitated by Howard's rare supremacy in both houses of parliament. Howard's economic inclinations had always made labour-market deregulation a key priority for him. His neo-liberal intentions were clear long before he became prime minister. On the very evening when he first became opposition leader in 1985 – over a decade before he would finally win an election – he made this plain: "I think the biggest economic challenge over the next five to ten years is to free up the labour market and in doing so alter the balance of our industrial-relations system."

From the moment of Howard's election victory, the conservative side of Australian politics – or at least its dominant party – had joined its British and American counterparts and decisively embraced the last radical progressive ideology of the twentieth century. History tells the story of an era of spectacular electoral success for conservatives at around this time. Howard's Coalition stayed in power for eleven years – the same as the Tories under Thatcher. Then, after Thatcher, came seven more years of Conservative rule. Reagan held power for the maximum eight years before handing over to another Republican president, George Bush Snr. Measured in such terms, neo-liberalism's heyday coincided with a golden age for conservative politics. But its implications for conservatism as a philosophy were far less auspicious. A new kind of conservatism was born: one that was a deeply ideological force in its own right and which had compromised some of the core principles of its own tradition. Conservatives were now on a neo-liberal-inspired crusade, or, to borrow from Reagan's speech to the British parliament, a "crusade for freedom that will engage the faith and fortitude of the next generation." Sure, there is something uniquely American about the style of rhetoric, but even so it is about as far away from Burke as you can get.

The trouble with neo-liberalism is that, like any revolutionary ideology, it does not easily translate into practice. It is one thing to privilege freedom over equality, but if the aim is to prevent the concentration of power, a problem soon arises, as financial inequality generates its own power concentrations. Similarly, it is one thing to decry the power of large corporations that tend towards monopoly, but it is altogether another for politicians promising a freer market with less state intervention to undertake the dismantling of mega-corporations and retain any credibility. Today, thanks largely to the global financial crisis, neo-liberalism is enduring the kind of scrutiny political orthodoxies usually don't receive. Analyses grind daily from the international commentariat explaining in morbid detail precisely how it is to blame for the risky, irresponsible and unregulated commercial practices that caused the global economy to dive. The intricacies of that debate are best left to far superior economic minds than mine, but it is important to note that so much of what ultimately transpired was more *laissez-faire* than it was truly neo-liberal. One of the global economy's gravest mistakes was that it permitted the creation of market monsters: the colossal investment banks that became "too big to fail." That should have been impossible in a neo-liberal world, where the very object is to prevent such concentrations of power. Indeed, this is exactly what Hayek abhorred in *laissez-faire* economics.

The invincibility of political imperatives means neo-liberalism was only ever going to find compromised expression. No national government was ever going to adopt Hayek's suggestion that the money supply should be denationalised and privatised. Margaret Thatcher was regularly criticised by neo-liberal think-tanks, such as the Institute of Economic Affairs and the Adam Smith Institute, for failing to go far enough in areas like town planning and especially agriculture, where Thatcher was accused of lending too much support to failing industries. Attempts to encourage new industries, like electronics, through subsidies were similarly derided as undue market intervention. While neo-liberal theorists obsessed over reduced government spending and balanced budgets, the largest budget deficits in American history occurred under two of that nation's most neo-liberal presidents: Reagan and George W. Bush (the latter even tried to privatise social security). Moreover, these presidencies did nothing to break down America's agricultural protectionism that has so enraged Australian farmers. At some junctures global free trade has been an ideal good enough for the powerless but not the powerful, which is certainly not the neo-liberal ideal.

America's neo-liberal era also facilitated the growth of mega-corporations, through legislation that removed limitations on the ways in which they could trade. The result has been the most staggering inequality America has known in about a century, and an associated concentration of power that has proven irresistible. America's various business lobbies are its most powerful, as Barack Obama has found out in his attempts to reform health care. Neo-liberalism lost any theoretical subtlety it had once had in the course of its political implementation. What had always had a radical streak suddenly became radioactive.

In the revolutionary atmosphere of Cold War victory, Western elites, many of whom were conservative politicians, immediately set about remaking the world in accordance with one version of the neo-liberal dream, starting with the former communist states. The very idea should have been absurd to a conservative, even one sympathetic to neo-liberalism in the West. A conservative knows that the free market works best when it has evolved naturally from the culture and institutions of the society in which it exists. This is why it has worked reasonably well in the Anglo-sphere. British society had made its transition from feudalism to a market-based economy by the eighteenth century. It had known early forms of capitalism for centuries and evolved a culture with individualist leanings. The free market is particularly suited to the United States, whose entire political edifice is built on the creed of individualism and individual liberty. Nothing could be less true of the former communist states, whose political inheritance was one of centralised political and economic authority and a more collectivist culture. Surely, if conservatism had one thing to teach us in that context, it was that an inorganic, externally constructed, global political revolution on neo-liberal lines was a project fraught with difficulty.

Gauging the success or otherwise of the subsequent transformation is a complex and ongoing process, but it is clear that it has not been the universal triumph that neo-liberal theory would lead us to expect. In his substantial body of analysis of post-Soviet economies, the US-based economist Peter Murrell argues that the most successful nations have been those where existing social and political forces were favourable to economic reform. For some countries, the transition remains a disappointment – at least according to those most affected by it. A 2003 study in Bulgaria found only about 15–20 per cent of the population have increased income, social mobility or consumption as a result of the transition from communism. A measly 5 per cent see themselves as having gained from it. That is not much of a record for an ideology that is meant to have solved every political conundrum. In a fascinating article for Prospect, Ivan Krastev provides an insight into why this might be the case, and predictably it has much to do with Bulgarian social structures. In the communist era, elites were restrained from behaving too conspicuously as such, and therefore had to enmesh themselves in society. That made them reliant to some degree in their daily lives on the cooperation of the downtrodden. Krastev explains:

Twenty years ago, even a member of the elite had to befriend his greengrocer if he wanted fresh fruit. He had to return a favour if the greengrocer asked him. In the perverse world of the shortage economy, the greengrocer decided who would get what. He was powerless and powerful at the same time. He "owned" the shop without taking the risks of real ownership. Corruption both eroded and sustained communism, by redistributing not only goods but also power. The exchange of favours unintentionally empowered the weak.

But, while the greengrocer benefited from the corruption of the communist system, he became the victim of the post-communist corruption. The revolution liberated him from having to decorate the shop with ideological nonsense. He gained the freedom to talk, to travel, to vote, to consume. But he lost his limited leverage over the elites. The power of the ballot is more abstract than the tangible influence he derived from his connections. Now there is no need for anybody to befriend the greengrocer to get fresh fruit. He cannot ask for favours from powerful customers.

The sweep of privatisation often placed business in the hands of a new elite. An ordinary communist-era shop owner probably lost his or her shop. If not, the taxes they paid have probably been replaced with payments to local criminals who have assumed a position of *de facto* authority. Krastev's point is not a pro-communist one. He does not pretend the greengrocer pines for a return to Soviet rule. But his analysis points to the unpredictable and often undesirable consequences that arise when the greatest wisdoms of conservatism are forgotten and a universalist ideology is introduced into a society with scant concern for the subtleties of local knowledge.

The result of all this neo-liberal idealism was a complete change in culture in the most powerful, global economic institutions, the IMF and the World Bank, under Reagan's influence. They originally operated as

Keynesian institutions, loaning money to nations lacking liquidity as a means of stimulating aggregate demand and avoiding economic downturns. That is to say, their role was to ensure global economic stability on the assumption that the market often did not work. Now they imbibed neo-liberalism's faith in markets as a universal organising principle. As a former chief economist at the World Bank, Joseph Stiglitz, would later confess in *Globalization and Its Discontents*, his organisation became so ideologically driven that empirical data often became irrelevant to its operations:

> When crises hit, the IMF prescribed outmoded, inappropriate, if "standard" solutions, without considering the effects they would have on the people in the countries told to follow these policies. Rarely did I see forecasts about what the policies would do to poverty. Rarely did I see thoughtful discussions and analyses of the consequences of alternative policies. There was a single prescription. Alternative opinions were not sought. Open, frank discussion was discouraged – there was no room for it. Ideology guided policy prescription and countries were expected to follow the IMF guidelines without debate.

It is difficult to imagine anything less conservative. At work here is an ideology that is contemptuous of local circumstances and local histories: the very thing that defines the conservative approach to social change. If conservatives are inclined to downplay the importance of debate (and they are often accused of avoiding it), it is because they place greater faith in custom and traditional institutions than they do in any abstract theory. Here the supreme ideology was radically changing the institutions in which it was operating. It is for this reason that many obituaries have been penned for traditional conservatism as a political philosophy since the commencement of the neo-liberal era. Here, for instance, in typically blistering style, is the conservative British philosopher John Gray:

The hegemony, within conservative thought and practice, of neo-liberal ideology has had the effect of destroying conservatism as a viable political project in our time and in any foreseeable future. Traditional conservatism is no longer a realistic political option when inherited institutions and practices have been swept away by the market forces which neo-liberal policies release or reinforce. When our institutional inheritance – that precious and irreplaceable patrimony of mediating structures and autonomous professions – is thrown away in the pursuit of a managerialist Cultural Revolution seeking to refashion the entire national life on the impoverished model of contract and market exchange, it is clear that the task of conserving and renewing a culture is no longer understood by contemporary conservatives.

THE CULTURAL REVOLUTION

Gray colourfully dubs neo-liberalism a "Maoism of the Right," a "permanent revolution of unfettered market processes, not the conservation of
traditional institutions and professions." It is this question of cultural
revolution that discussions of neo-liberalism so often overlook, but which
should be central to any conservative analysis. The basic components of
it are familiar enough in our public discourse: our society has become
increasingly atomised and individualist; community life is breaking
down as people's working lives become more irregular, mobile and
incompatible with sustained and continuous community activity; families
are suffering as a result of the same working irregularities and the need
for everyone in the family to work in order to maintain the kinds of life-
styles society now demands. The very logic of this makes a mockery of
any conservative pretence to "family values."

The market society is one of constant, rapid change. Workplaces are
regularly undergoing mergers, downsizings or restructuring. Unemployment may decrease, but security does not increase with it, because the
traditional link between jobs and social stability has been severed. The
workforce is becoming increasingly casualised and dispensable, or, to use
the neo-liberal euphemism, "flexible." Lives are becoming increasingly
mobile as working life demands it. Precisely as neo-liberal theory predicts,
this is a working life devoid of such archaic concepts as loyalty, for what
place does loyalty have in a society of individual entrepreneurs?

No doubt this is dynamic. No doubt it has considerable charm, particularly for those of us who are winners from this process, on whom it con-
fers increased choice and control over our lives. But is it conservative? It
is difficult to imagine how it might be, unless of course conservatism is
radically redefined. As the rapidly increasing inequalities of neo-liberalism
in practice demonstrate, the winners from such arrangements are a comparatively small elite. For many others it means heightened uncertainty
and insecurity, which should surely be of great conservative concern.

The idea that we should be pursuing constant economic advancement without serious regard for people's sense of their own security sounds very much like the utopian politics of progressivism.

For conservatives like Gray, the social consequences have been predictably depressing. He cites the spike in crime in Britain as an example, flowing from the collapse of community life and the corresponding disintegration of informal mechanisms for regulating social behaviour. Neoliberal ideologues, he concedes, would ridicule such a diagnosis. They blame the welfare state as the cause of such anti-social behaviour, on the basis that welfare creates a disincentive to more productive pursuits. But, counters Gray (who is no fan of the welfare state), this ignores the fact that higher levels of crime have always prevailed in individualist America than in welfare-bound Britain. The key factor, it seems, is not levels of welfare but norms of behaviour implicit in culture and custom.

The problem is an increasingly familiar one to Australians facing their own spike in violent crime and drunkenness. There is also good empirical evidence comparing communities in Britain and the United States to show a strong relationship between high levels of inequality and high levels of violent crime. The associated theory is that violence is an expression of insecurity and that rampant inequality exacerbates this. But these are heretical connections to draw, particularly for today's conservative politicians, because they interrogate the social consequences of their neoliberal-inspired dogma. In all likelihood, owing to the ideological workings of political discourse, those advancing such arguments will be dismissed as leftist, or even Marxist: they do not side with the right "team." In fact, such arguments are quite traditionally conservative, particularly as articulated by the emphatically anti-Marxist Gray.

What, exactly, is the social idea that binds together this new kind of society? For Hayek it was the market, but that does not exactly make for a compelling narrative in human terms. The supreme cultural value here is consumer preference and autonomy. This sort of social template is powerless to respond to any of the social monstrosities it throws up. In October

2006, the Australia Institute issued a discussion paper highlighting the increasing frequency of "corporate paedophilia": the sexualisation of children in advertising and marketing. The phenomenon takes several forms: there is the celebration of overt adult sexuality in children's magazines, where readers are encouraged to develop crushes on celebrities or imitate sexualised dance routines on the music videos of female artists like The Veronicas or Rihanna. Alternatively, children themselves (particularly girls) are depicted in sexualised ways, in skimpy clothing with hot pink lipstick striking provocative poses that would be all hips and breasts if they were old enough to have them. No parent with young girls needed a study to confirm this: a browse through the children's clothing aisles will quickly do the job. Girls as young as two can get around in a pair of knickers with "Heaven Scent" emblazoned on the crotch. We have G-strings for five-year-olds and T-shirts that scream "So many boys, so little time." Forget My Little Pony. Meet the Bratz dolls with their bikinis, hot pants, fishnet stockings and feather boas. Even Barbie is a prude now. In a few years' time these same girls can buy T-shirts bearing such hilarious new Mr Men characters as "Miss Floozy," "Mr Pimp," "Mr Drunk" and "Mr Well Hung." The consequences of this are well rehearsed by child and adolescent psychologists: low self-esteem, depression, anorexia, crises of body image leading to eating disorders and, of course, underage sex, which might explain why there were more than 40,000 teenage abortions in England and Wales in 2006, nearly 4000 of which were for girls under sixteen.

Corporate paedophilia, explains the discussion paper, is a metaphor that "encapsulates the idea that such advertising and marketing is an abuse both of children and of public morality." The Australia Institute is often described as advocating from the Left, but it should be conservatives making this kind of argument. Public morality? That sounds like the quintessential conservative concern. And yet the nation's conservative broadsheet could find in this only a "moral panic." Staggeringly, it editorialised that "sexuality is in the eye of the beholder," blaming the report's authors for reading sexual content into "an innocent picture of a child."

Note, though, the editorial's line of attack: the whole report was simply the conjuring of "a hardline feminist working at an anti-free market think-tank." Here is the crux of the matter. Never mind the serious issue of cultural disintegration at hand, this was an attack on the free market, and therefore heresy. The problem inevitably had to be dismissed as the ideologically driven overstatement of a raving anti-capitalist – a complaint from the Left.

Even if we assume the report was the work of the most radically committed Marxists, it is telling that the conservative commentator could see only neo-liberal ideological warfare. It is characteristic of the way conservatism has snookered itself behind neo-liberalism's eight-ball that its representatives cannot recognise a clear conservative cause even when presented with one. Sure, as the editorial urged, parents bear some responsibility for protecting their children from such exploitation. But it is a highly artificial – and deeply un-conservative – view both of society and human nature to assume the matter ends there; that people are so independent of their environment that they can remain wholly unaffected by the onslaught of advertising. About the only cultural analysis the editorial could offer was that "the crass sexualisation of society was kicked off by the Left, which in one generation overturned centuries of Western tradition and taboos with its 'anything goes' agenda." It was a feeble response for three obvious reasons. First, it is unclear precisely in what way the sexual revolution implied the sexualisation of children. Second, the sexual revolution was in the 1960s. If this ultimately is the sole cause of the problem, it is difficult to see why it took three or four decades to express itself. Third and most importantly, the issue here is the commercial exploitation of sexuality. Even if the Left is supposed to be comfortable with this kind of sexualisation and is seeking to propagate it, that does not remotely explain why any conservative should defend a social structure which seeks to trade on it.

In fact, such sexualisation is an entirely predictable consequence of neo-liberal logic. Such dross exists because it is profitable. The market has determined that it shall have a place in society, and because the market is the new dominant political rationality, there is no conservative answer to this claim. Yet the problem is not the concept of the free market *per se*. A conservative need not be a staunch isolationist or protectionist, and few would doubt that some economic rethinking had become necessary by the end of the 1970s. Rather the problem is one of philosophical priority. Do markets exist in the service of people and communities, or does society exist to facilitate the market? Are markets intended to operate as an expression of underlying social norms and culture, or do they determine them? Is perpetual economic growth (leaving aside its impossibility for a moment) the very purpose of politics, or is it merely one factor in determining the health of a society and the quality of life of its people? A politics that views markets as a means rather than an end is more likely to see principled intervention as necessary – that is, to impose political constraints on the market's operation. It is more likely to come up with concrete ways, for example, of resisting the odious sexualisation of children, not because it is efficient, but because it is necessary in and of itself. Similarly, to take an example of great political moment, it is more likely to restrain the market's degradation of the environment on the basis that this is more important than continued efficiency.

It is one of the ironies of Australia's neo-liberalisation through the 1980s that the Labor Party seems to have had a stronger grasp of its social implications than its conservative opponents. The Hawke and Keating governments understood that for the globalisation and deregulation of Australia's economy to go well, significant *cultural* change would be required. In 1989, Hawke's economic adviser Ross Garnaut published a report, *Australia and the North-East Asian Ascendancy*, in which he advocated rapid economic integration with Asia. In basic trading terms that meant Australia should increase its exports in aluminium, wool and steel, while dropping its tariffs rapidly to encourage greater foreign investment from the region. This in turn meant the integration of Australia's *people* with those of Asia.

Australia would need a higher intake of Asian immigrants; it would need to receive more Asian investors and tourists; numbers of Asian students would increase, as would the influx of Asian businesspeople, professionals, entrepreneurs and property owners. If Australia was going to trade with Asia, it had to become *of* Asia. This included the introduction of compulsory Asian history and language courses in schools and the forging of links between Australian and Asian tertiary institutions. Not all of this became government policy, but much of it did.

This Asian leaning, begun under Hawke, became a centrepiece of Keating's cultural politics, along with two other elements: reconciliation with the indigenous population and the push for a republic. As Paul Kelly observed in *The End of Certainty*, Keating set out to remake the very foundations of Australian culture and identity. These had begun to erode anyway under the Whitlam and Fraser governments through the renunciation of the White Australia policy and the adoption of multi-culturalism, but Keating's cultural narrative was more comprehensive. A globalised economy with globalised industries running globalised workplaces signals a new cosmopolitan order. White Australia, of course, had to be abandoned as an ideal, but the implicit cultural transformation was more sweeping. Australia's British inheritance was of decreasing value in a global, and especially an Asian, context. Australia therefore had to say goodbye to an identity as an imperial beneficiary. The brave new neo-liberal world was not one in which Britain would look after Australia's economic interests, and neither would its geo-political succes-sor, the United States. Australian society must embrace an independent identity, which has obvious republican implications. That new identity would be based on its new position within the global market society. Australia would necessarily become more culturally diverse as it filled with individual entrepreneurs from all over the world, especially from our home region.

This is not exactly a conservative course of action, but then, neither Hawke nor Keating were on the conservative side of party politics. The

Coalition, meanwhile, struggled to find a response. The trouble started in earnest around 1984 when the conservative historian Geoffrey Blainey began a trenchant campaign against Australia's increased levels of Asian immigration, declaring that it was tantamount to surrendering Australia. Asian immigrants were highly conspicuous in Australian society and this would cause great social hardship for them and for the host society. Accordingly, the rate of Asian immigration had to be slowed and multiculturalism abandoned in the interests of social cohesion. The Liberal Party's shadow immigration minister, Michael Hodgman, immediately ran with the theme, accusing Labor of compromising Australia's heritage by greatly reducing British and European migration. The party's leader at the time, Andrew Peacock, began to echo the sentiment, though in more moderate language. Peacock's strategy was not to argue for cuts to Asian immigration, but for a boost from Europe. His stance led to media accusations of racist politics and caused a major rift within the party. Ian Macphee, who as immigration minister under Fraser had overseen increases in Asian immigration and the early days of Australian multi-culturalism, fiercely protested against Peacock and Hodgman's position. He lamented the debate, which had "fuelled some anti-Asian sentiment that is tragic for this country." Eventually the matter was resolved by rejection of Blainey's argument and a return to the Fraser government's immigra-tion policy. John Howard had agreed with some of Blainey's concerns but ultimately rejected restrictions on Asian immigration along with his party. A few years later, though, he signalled a return to the Blainey position, infamously expressing his reservations about levels of Asian immigration and recommending they be either left unchanged or slowed. It was a position that cost Howard the Liberal Party leadership, and which he ultimately had to repudiate in order to reclaim it several years later.

Hawke held firm the whole time, refusing to take Australia back to a discriminatory immigration policy. In a significant speech before the House of Representatives, he explained the basis of his conviction:

There are very few things that one can be certain of in life when we are talking in the field of economics. But there is one thing that we can be certain of when we are talking about the economic future of this country; that is, that the future wellbeing, the future development, the future capacity for growth, the future capacity for improving living standards in this country, is to be seen in terms of the fact that we must become and we will inevitably become more enmeshed in the region of which we are a part. We are a country of just over 15 million people in a world of seven and a half billion, but in a region of billions of people. We have to understand as Australians that that is where our future lies. It is where our capacity to provide a better life for our children and their children lies. Therefore, anything that this country does which is in fact or which is seen to be in terms of prejudice against that region would be not only immoral but also manifestly against the present and future best interests of the people of this country.

The crucial point, so often neglected in the story of the cultural politics of the Hawke–Keating governments, is that this politics was entirely consistent with, and indeed implicit in, their philosophy of economic liberalisation. It was not merely a feel-good construction of leftist elites pursuing their own cosmopolitan fantasies, but a logical extension of neo-liberalism's inherently globalising dynamic. Keating's world was very much in tune with Hayek's "One World" theorising. To be sure, it was a radical change for the Labor Party, for so long the party of the cultural and economic protection of White Australia, but it is also the kind of transition one can make from a starting point of progressive politics. If cultural dispositions were not compatible with necessary reforms, they needed to be remade. That immediately sounds more neo-liberal than conservative. The coalition's courting of anti-Asian sentiment in the electorate only lent force to the impression that, in Paul Kelly's words, it was "weak on the social and cultural changes without which free market economics and Asia/Pacific integration could not be achieved."

It is too easy to dismiss these conservative social concerns as an expression of rank racism. Undoubtedly the politics of xenophobia played a part, but the more restrained elements of the debate were an entirely legitimate expression of conservative political thought. That fact, however, only discloses a philosophical inconsistency that has bedevilled conservative politics ever since. It is fine to stand for social and cultural continuities, but not after signing up to the radical social reconstruction of neo-liberalism. On that basis, we can possibly excuse the scepticism concerning Asian immigration in the mid-1980s, when the wet/dry debate was still very much alive, but the intra-party victory of economic rationalism through the medium of John Howard surely ends any such dispensation.

Revolutionary change is, by its nature, irreversible. Having unleashed the radically transformative power of the free market, conservatism has no plausible option of retreat. The defenders of tradition have become apologists for radical change, and cultural norms and old habits of living have no axiomatic purchase in this new social environment. Everything is up for grabs, or, more tellingly, for sale. Neo-liberalism is resolutely progressive: it promises ongoing economic growth and unending social change in the pursuit of perfect liberty. It precipitates a cultural world in perpetual and rapid flux, meaning culture and society are always in an accelerated process of becoming something else. That sort of environment – created in large part by conservative politicians – renders the social and cultural aspects of traditional conservatism a nullity.

That is not to say conservatives have accepted this fact. With the exception of a minority of conservative voices who have long warned of conservatism's incompatibility with neo-liberalism, they haven't. Their ideological commitment to the market has blinded them to its more catastrophic possibilities, and also to its social implications. Instead, when culture fragments and atomises as inevitably it must in a neo-liberal environment, conservatives have found themselves resorting to a new brand of cultural politics in a vain attempt to restore the balance. Hereabouts "culture wars" and shrill forms of nationalism often appear – what Gray calls a "cultural fundamentalism" that is not truly conservative, but rather nostalgic: pining for a past social stability and coherence that is no longer feasible. At an extreme this became manifest in the striking rise of European ultra-nationalist parties through the 1990s and 2000s: the Freedom Party in Austria, the Flemish Block in Belgium, the Danish People's Party, Jean-Marie Le Pen's National Front in France, the Northern League in Italy, Pim Fortuyn's List in the Netherlands, Norway's Progress Party, the Popular Party in Portugal, the British National Party – and of course, Australia's One Nation. In several cases (Norway, Italy, the Netherlands, Denmark) these often openly racist parties rose to the level of being in a ruling coalition. That does not mean they captured the conservative mainstream, but they certainly exerted a substantial gravitational pull. Neo-liberal parties either followed the lead or were moving in a similarly atavistic direction. The resultant discourse is by now a very familiar one: tough on immigrants and laden with values talk. So it is that the Conservative British prime minister John Major launched his shambolic "Back to Basics" campaign, calling for the rediscovery of old values like "self-discipline" and "consideration for others." The campaign fell apart quickly after a slew of Tories became embroiled in sordid sex scandals, but it was philosophically doomed from the beginning. Neo-liberal politics has almost nothing to do with self-discipline and consideration for others. It is designed on assumptions of unlimited desire and individualist ambition.

Such developments are scarcely surprising. The point is that neo-liberalism's *Homo economicus* is a fiction. The very thing that has made conservatism such a valuable and enduring political resource for centuries is that it rejects such one-dimensional understandings of human nature and the political dreams built on them. Eroding the social order was always going to precipitate a visceral response. Keynes was right in at least one very important respect: throughout history, belligerent forms of cultural politics have tended to emerge from moments of insecurity. And so it is that the insecurities inherent in neo-liberal globalisation have revitalised those twin forms of cultural belligerence: ultra-nationalism and religious fundamentalism. The rising popularity of these convictions is not coincidental. Both are perfectly suited to neo-liberal times because they provide precisely what is missing: continuity, groundedness, stability, a sense of historicity. It matters not that the worldview they promote is quite recently invented rather than authentic. Provided it speaks the language of tradition, it offers something increasingly rare in a market society. If people cannot find a sense of security themselves through shared social norms, they will do so through the politics of identity.

It is something to be mourned that this is the most conservatism can muster now: a new version of itself built on the contradictory impulses of neo-liberalism and a strident cultural politics. Alas, ideological consistency is a rare political virtue. Rather than vacate the social realm as neo-liberalism would have them do, conservatives have found themselves attempting very much the opposite. Conservatives, of course, have a natural interest in culture. But this modern brand of cultural politics is something altogether different, because it is a means of overcompensating for the radical social forces it has unleashed. It is therefore destined to be reactionary rather than principled. This new conservatism is ideologically driven, but not ideologically consistent. It is belligerent and rhetorically clear, but it is not coherent.

I am going to call this new conservatism "neo-conservatism." Here, I should be clear that I do not intend this term in its narrow, American sense, referring only to those foreign-policy thinkers that are often thought to have dominated the thinking of President George W. Bush. No doubt that strand of thinking – populated, instructively, by former Marxists and Trotskyists – is a very significant strand in the neo-conservatism I am describing, but I use the term here in a more generic, international sense that is not confined to utopian foreign-policy designs. Here, it denotes the mutated conservatism that rose to prominence during the neo-liberal era, starting in the 1970s. It was visible to varying degrees in the politics of Thatcher, Reagan and, of course, George W. Bush, but for Australian purposes its most seminal exponent was John Howard. Howard famously described himself as the most conservative leader the Liberal Party has ever had. Judged by the tradition of conservative political philosophy, however, it becomes possible to see precisely the opposite: that Howard was not particularly conservative at all, and that to the extent he was, he was neo-conservative. This is a crucial idea to understand because it explains a great deal about the state of Australian conservatism today.

There are several places we might look for illustrations of this neo-conservatism and its sharp departure from the liberal conservative tradition. As we have seen, the Iraq war is undoubtedly one of them. In this essay, however, I am going to draw upon neo-conservative approaches to multiculturalism, which have loomed large in recent years. My intention here is not to defend the policy of multiculturalism (which I support but accept is open to critique), but to demonstrate that neo-conservatism does not respond to it on respectable liberal conservative grounds. Instead, it counters with a reactionary form of monoculturalism that violates the first principles of the liberal conservative tradition.

US AND THEM

At the heart of neo-conservatism is a sense of siege. It is inclined to speak in near-conspiratorial terms about the ideological terrain that confronts it. In America, where both neo-conservatism and neo-liberalism have had their purest expression, this became apparent in the mid-1970s, when arch neo-conservative Irving Kristol warned of a creeping "new class" whose members are "not much interested in money but are keenly interested in power," specifically

> the power to shape our civilization – a power, which, in a capitalist system, is supposed to reside in the free market. The 'new class' wants to see much of this power redistributed to government where they will then have a major say in how it is exercised.

The "new class" is apparently a very broad one, consisting of "a goodly proportion of those college-educated people," namely

> scientists, teachers and educational administrators, journalists and others in the communication industries, psychologists, social workers, those lawyers and doctors who make their careers in the expanding public sector, city planners, the staffs of the larger foundations, the upper levels of the government bureaucracy.

Kristol, a former Trotskyist, had constructed a new "class war" between this "new class" and what would come later to be called the nation's "moral majority." Since the beginning, then, American neo-conservatism has been obsessed with the agenda of "liberal elites" who exploit their privileged position to indoctrinate the nation and take it over with their anti-capitalism. Particular venom in this connection is saved for the "liberal media," which is blamed for everything from spreading the myth of global warming to derailing the vice-presidential campaign of Sarah Palin and delivering Barack Obama the presidency.

The discourse of Australian neo-conservatism is essentially the same, provided one substitutes for the uniquely American misuse of "liberal" the terms "leftist," "inner-city" or "latte-sipping." One of the most conspicuous features of Howard's social politics was his prosecution of the culture and history wars. The components of the "new class" are all there: civil-liberties lawyers, (particularly climate) scientists, academics. The narrative – promulgated by both Howard and his devotees in the commentariat – was that Australian cultural institutions and the telling of Australian history had been captured by a leftist orthodoxy spreading a "black armband" version of Australian history that emphasised, exaggerated and even distorted the atrocities of colonial violence against the indigenous population. This in turn precipitated cultural relativism and an obsession with political correctness. At fault were the proliferation of special-interest groups, leftist academics and, of course, a biased media. On this last point, the ABC was particularly pilloried.

Consistent with neo-conservative ambition, Howard's approach was not merely restorative. Neo-conservatism, after all, is concerned with vanquishing ideological foes. Accordingly, Howard undertook the very project he so despised in his leftist foes, promoting what we might call, in the prevailing spirit of trench warfare, a Right orthodoxy on history and culture. Australia's history was "heroic," its "blemishes" insufficient to negate its net positive "balance sheet." Meanwhile he articulated a new Australian mythology centred on military history: Anzac Day, once a fading reference point, was reinvigorated to the point of national definition. Howard was even prepared to use notionally apolitical appointments for such political ends. Most famously, this involved appointing ideologically friendly figures to the boards of influential cultural institutions, especially the National Museum and the troublesome ABC. Harry Evans, the fiercely non-partisan former Clerk of the Senate, argued that the Howard government seemed surprisingly dismissive of the checks and balances in Australia's parliamentary institutions. Its failed attempt in 2003 to change the conditions for joint sittings, for instance, would have transferred considerable power from the parliament to the executive.

These sorts of behaviour only confirm the ideological content of neo-conservatism, as distinct from traditional conservatism's focus on institutional integrity. As Judith Brett observed in her book *Australian Liberals and the Moral Middle Class*, no other conservative leader in Australia had embarked on this sort of cultural program. Constructing orthodox narratives was the stuff of progressive politics; conservatives spoke more about order, the sanctity of institutions and the Queen.

The neo-conservative approach to cultural diversity fits within this broader political project of forging a new national orthodoxy on culture in the face of a relentless siege. Multiculturalism – part of the leftist cultural takeover – is predictably a large target, on the grounds that it surrenders society to cultural relativism and the decay of values; that it risks raising tolerance to the level of what an editorial in the *Australian* so cheerfully called "a cultural suicide pact." On this view, multiculturalism is a policy that has assumed the status of a political ideology. The neo-conservative response, though, is to produce a counter-ideology of its own: mono-culturalism. Sometimes this is expressed through the language of integration, at other times through the more honest language of assimilation, where an approved version of the "majority culture" is asserted as something with which minorities must reconcile themselves.

This argument proceeds from two quite divergent assumptions. The first, as we have seen, is that the cultural revolution of the Left has destroyed the moral integrity of society in favour of postmodern cultural relativism. In the words of Melanie Phillips, a British neo-conservative feted in Australia by the conservative establishment (and who, like many neo-conservatives, describes herself as once left-wing), the result has been "the creation of a debauched and disorderly culture of instant gratification, with disintegrating families, feral children and violence, squalor and vulgarity on the streets." This civilisational decay has created a vacuum into which assertive minorities have marched, refusing to alter their behaviour because all cultures must be treated as equally valid. Neo-conservatives add to this a second belief that there still exists a majority culture which is to remain supreme, and to which minorities (and especially migrants) must accordingly submit themselves. It is a curious coupling, which requires migrants to assimilate into a culture that, thanks to the leftist, postmodern cultural revolution, has apparently already been relativised to the point of destruction.

Such arguments took on a special urgency when the threat of terrorism dominated public discourse. In this regard the key turning point was not the attacks of 11 September 2001 but the London bombings in July 2005, which were carried out by four young people, all British citizens, all raised in Britain and three of them born there. A connection between the capitulation of majority culture before advancing, aggressive minorities, and Islamist terrorism came swiftly to be drawn in terms that were, frankly, apocalyptic. Through multiculturalism, Western culture had completely surrendered itself to the politics of separatism, which has in turn nurtured nothing less than terrorist agents within. The West's very survival is precarious both physically and culturally, and multiculturalism is to blame. Migrants therefore need to be told how to behave. They must, to quote Phillips again, "accept minority status." Left to their own devices – or worse, invited to retain their cultural identities – they will proceed disastrously to inflict their backward cultures on the majority. Assimilation is therefore urgent. The alternative is, as the *Australian* editorialised, that "immigrants ... behave as conquerors." The very future of liberal society, and even liberal democracy, is imperilled.

The Howard government took this seriously, embarking on an extensive and often belligerent "Australian values" campaign that encompassed both government policy and rhetoric. Given the circumstances in which it arose, it often took Muslims as its focus. In August 2005, Bronwyn Bishop advocated the banning of headscarves in state schools on the basis that such clothing was being used as "a sort of iconic item of defiance" by "the sort of people who want to overturn our values." Howard politely declined the suggestion, describing it as "impractical" since it would have to apply also to turbans and yarmulkes, before adding, almost as an afterthought, that the idea was also not "desirable." Even so, he took the opportunity to expand the discussion a few months later on talkback radio, saying, "I don't believe you should ban wearing headscarves, but I do think the full garb is confronting and that is how most people feel."

At about the same time as Bishop, the then education minister, Brendan Nelson, declared remarkably that Muslims who "don't want to live by Australian values" should simply "clear off." Those values remained unspecified, but they were apparently embodied in the Anzac legend of Simpson and his donkey, dodging gunfire and rescuing injured diggers at Gallipoli. It was perhaps the most belligerent ministerial comment towards a sector of the electorate in living memory. Earlier in the same week, Peter Costello said basically the same thing, then reiterated it the following year in a speech at the Sydney Institute that also castigated the prevailing "mushy, misguided multiculturalism." John Howard, meanwhile, asserted the government's right to monitor mosques and Islamic schools to prevent terrorism, saying that "if people are not willing to give their first loyalty to this country, they obviously must understand that that will arouse enormous concern within the rest of the Australian community."

So there was little surprise when the Howard government famously dropped the phrase "multicultural affairs" from the name of the relevant government department. It instituted citizenship tests to require migrants to learn the English language, Australian history and Australian values. This, of course, accompanied continuous governmental injunctions that Muslims integrate, which for Howard "means accepting Australian values" such as "the equality of men and women."

More examples could easily be adduced here (for there are countless on which to draw), but the rhetorical pattern is clear. The purpose of this essay is not to survey them extensively or even to evaluate their merits in any great detail (I have done that elsewhere). For present purposes this neo-conservative approach to cultural politics is relevant because of its sharp divergence from the principles of the liberal conservative tradition.

Indeed, there is something vaguely paradoxical in the whole discourse. Not only do minorities fume violently at values that have allegedly been destroyed, but the neo-conservative solution is to enforce conformity with those values in the ostensible defence of liberal democracy. It is a mind-bending prescription. As we have seen, an inescapable implication of liberalism is the individual's freedom of thought. That means nothing if it does not permit the individual to subscribe to dissenting value systems that may even be repugnant to the majority – just as freedom of speech means nothing without the freedom to offend. As Mill emphasised in *On Liberty*:

> The appropriate region of human liberty ... comprises, first, the inward domain of consciousness; demanding liberty of conscience in the most comprehensive sense; liberty of thought and feeling; absolute freedom of opinion and sentiment on all subjects, practical or speculative, scientific, moral, or theological.

Neo-conservatism discloses its divergence from traditional liberalism at the moment when it embarks upon the project of commanding minority compliance with majority culture. For neo-conservatives, people must be assimilated into what it declares to be the mainstream (and note here the neo-conservative tendency to say with utter confidence what the majority thinks). Liberalism is precisely about the protection of individuals *outside* the mainstream. It is emphatically *anti*-majoritarian. For the traditional liberal, when majority culture is enforced by the institutions of the State, it becomes mere ossified custom, which is precisely what Mill considered so despotic. Mill feared the tyranny of the majority and argued that where society "issues wrong mandates instead of right, or any mandates at all in things with which it ought not to meddle, it practises a social tyranny more formidable than many kinds of political oppression." The fact remains that "if all mankind minus one were of one opinion, and only one person were of the contrary opinion, mankind would be no more justified in silencing that one person, than he, if he had the power, would be justified in silencing mankind." We have seen similar concerns expressed within the conservative tradition by thinkers such as Lecky and de Tocqueville, who feared democracy on the basis that majoritarian politics would compromise liberty. As noted above, liberalism's values are institutional: the rule of law, freedom of speech and conscience. It has no interest in intervening until the law is breached, and it does not use the law as a means of mandating a majority culture.

This does not imply that the State is utterly relativist. A liberal state may well reflect and even privilege one set of cultural norms over another. It is perfectly entitled to use an official language, or to choose for public recognition certain days of national significance. It is not illiberal to mark Anzac Day, or Remembrance Day, or to make Christmas a public holiday. Similarly, the liberal State is not bound to legalise female genital mutilation simply because it is practised within some cultures. In fact, it is bound to prohibit it – especially on children – in accordance with the harm principle. But a liberal State does not seek to prescribe or determine the personal values of its citizens. It does not require its citizens to like Anzac Day (or even Simpson and his donkey). It may well restrain an employer from engaging in sexual discrimination on the basis that it restricts the freedom of others, but it does not lecture the employer on the need to relinquish his or her sexist convictions. If people want to cherish a barbaric custom such as female genital mutilation, the liberal State has nothing to say. If they practise it, they are placed in prison because they have inflicted clear, demonstrable harm on another person. Until the law turns to legalising that sort of behaviour – which it simply will never do – there should be no existential crisis for liberal democracy on the basis of its citizens' values. Recall that impeccably liberal passage from John Howard's 1997 Australia Day speech, quoted earlier:

> The beliefs that we have about what it is to be an Australian are
> not things that can be imposed from above by political leaders of
> any persuasion. They are not things that can be generated by [a]

self-appointed cultural elite who seek to tell us what our identity ought to be ... Our identity ... is never something that can be imposed.

And yet, here was a government led by an ostensibly liberal political party doing precisely that: telling the people what it means to be Australian, demanding that its citizens accept certain (often unspecified) values, denying citizenship to people who could not learn to regurgitate them in an English-language test, requiring citizens to identify with their nation before anything else, and thereby deciding their identity for them. The inherent contradictions in this were neatly captured in one passage, often echoed by Howard, during Brendan Nelson's Simpson's donkey harangue:

> We don't care where people come from; we don't mind what religion they've got or what their particular view of the world is. But if you want to be in Australia, if you want to raise your children in Australia, we fully expect those children to be taught and to accept Australian values and beliefs.

Note the philosophical shift mid-way. The statement is in two contradictory halves. When speaking broadly in terms of principle, the discourse is liberal. The minute it comes to application, it is illiberal and neo-conservative. We don't care what your view of the world is, but you must accept Australian values and beliefs. Believe anything you want, provided it is what we say defines Australianness. There, in miniature, is the first dimension of neo-conservatism's abandonment of Mill.

To be sure, that abandonment was not comprehensive. The Howard government, for instance, never attacked Rupert Murdoch for surrendering his Australian citizenship and becoming an American in order to pursue his business interests there – not even when the *Bulletin* named him the most influential Australian of all time. And no one seemed to note the irony when, upon accepting that award, he warned that Muslims would never put their national identity first. Of course, neo-liberal logic was firmly on Murdoch's side. He had abandoned the tangible representation of his national identity for entrepreneurial reasons. He was *Homo economicus* before he was *Homo Australis*, but it didn't seem to matter. Of course, Murdoch is too powerful to be bullied in this way, but this also demonstrates that Howard's neo-conservative cultural politics was concerned only with those that threatened the cultural orthodoxy he sought to impose. It was, therefore, ideological. Murdoch was not threatening that.

Neither, it seems, were the Exclusive Brethren, a Christian sect that confounded the Howard government's emphasis on Australian values. According to news reports, they shunned democracy to the extent that they forbade voting. They shunned non-believers, requiring members to avoid conversation with them, and they were prepared to separate children from parents if necessary. They shunned university education. They protected men who were convicted of sexually abusing young girls, and they vandalised the homes of those bringing the charges. They required their women to wear long, loose-fitting clothes. They flouted court orders. In short, they rejected such well-rehearsed Australian values as democracy, the rule of law, gender equality and tolerance, and certainly integration. Yet the values-promoting prime minister not only refrained from lecturing this sect on integration, he also repeatedly met with its members, while his party benefited from its donations. When pressed on this, John Howard remarked, "It's a free country … and they were not breaking the law." And, of course, aside from the fact that they were alleged to have broken the law by violating court orders, and that the government was alleged to have been receiving money from them, Howard's statement of principle was perfectly correct from a liberal point of view. In a free (that is, liberal) country, the government has no concern with the beliefs of its citizens if they are not breaking the law. That is as true for the Exclusive Brethren as it is for Muslims who do not speak English.

Pluralism is a necessary consequence of liberalism. Cultural pluralism, therefore, is something that liberalism is bound to accept, provided it arises without State coercion. This does not mean multiculturalism is liberalism's necessary logical extension, or that liberal conservatives are bound by principle to embrace it. As we have seen, liberalism conceives of the relationship between the State and the citizen on the basis that the citizen is an individual. While accepting cultural diversity, liberalism may therefore quite plausibly object to a State policy of multiculturalism on the ground that the state should engage with citizens as individuals, rather than as members of a cultural group. The *Australian*'s Janet Albrechtsen mounts precisely this argument, and it is a cogent one: "It's time for our political leaders to stop engaging with Muslims as Muslims," she writes. "They are citizens; no special rules apply."

Much the same way as such liberal individualism informed Howard's approach to indigenous affairs, it informed his opposition to multiculturalism. Indeed, even well before his prime ministership, this was the very basis of his objection. His *Future Directions* manifesto from 1988 criticises multiculturalism because its result will be to "ensnare individuals in ethnic communities denying them the opportunity to fully participate in Australian society." While it is true that a liberal argument for multiculturalism can also be mounted – on the basis that an individual is entitled to their cultural group affiliation – Howard's was a perfectly respectable liberal position to hold.

The problem is that neo-conservatism's cultural crusade prevents this principle from being applied consistently. So Albrechtsen also applauds when the government outlines for Muslims – specifically as Muslims – which personal values they must accept. Of course it is true that values are critically important to society, for it could scarcely exist without them. Indeed, that is a very good, conservative reason for rejecting neo-liberalism. But if values are to be promoted within the framework of liberalism, they are not the stuff of government declaration and should not be articulated in group terms.

Yet the cultural politics of neo-conservatism very quickly resort to a kind of groupism, prosecuting an identity politics of collectivism. The neo-conservative desire that minorities know their place, that they understand they are minorities and behave as such, reveals a collectivist instinct. Should we not be apprehending them as individual citizens? Take, as another example, Peter Costello's Sydney Institute discussion of the Danish cartoons controversy:

> I do not like putrid representations like *Piss Christ*. I do not think galleries should show them. But I do recognise they should be able to practise their offensive taste without fear of violence or a riot. Muslims do not like representation of the Prophet. They do not think newspapers should print them. But so too they must recognize this does not justify violence against newspapers, or countries that allow newspapers to publish them.

All true enough, but why say it? Had Muslims in Australia been torching media outlets and embassies? The concealed fact here is that there was almost no response at all in Australia to the cartoons, although the *Courier-Mail* reproduced the most offensive of them. Costello ignored this, preferring instead to invoke the performance of mobs in places of already heightened political tension, such as Syria or Gaza. Australian Muslims become guilty by fabricated association. Here they are not only treated as a group, but as a global one, saddled with the conduct of antipodean co-religionists they have probably never met and whose circumstances are wildly different. Their individual agency is denied.

Coming from those who apparently champion liberalism, this is evidence of an intriguing tension. It demonstrates that the new neo-liberal neo-conservatism is not simply the dispassionate application of a political philosophy. It is philosophically inconsistent, even though it is ideologically passionate. It is instead a reactionary, combative doctrine that seeks out enemies it can destroy. In the black and white world of neo-conservatism, there are, ultimately, those who belong and those who do not; those who are with us, and those who are against us. This is neither a liberal outlook, nor a conservative one.

It is true, of course, that the desire to preserve and protect cultural forms is a conservative instinct. Neo-conservative culture wars therefore appear superficially conservative in the sense that they claim to be defensive of a long-established cultural edifice. But to argue this point is to ignore that it is driven by the trench warfare of Left/Right politics. So much of the assimilatory values talk of neo-conservatism is addressed to immigrant minorities, but it is not truly about them. Minorities are just rhetorical pawns in the game against the leftist new class. This is a political performance for the majority. By articulating the values that migrants threaten, neo-conservatives articulate those that the majority is deemed to accept. Howard's persistent speaking for the national "mainstream" reinforced the idea that those who disagreed were not fully of the nation. This is not, therefore, a narrative of national unity, as was so often advertised. It was a narrative of exclusion. It is about the power to define a dominant culture.

In neo-liberal times, that is a vain hope indeed. Never before has culture been less fixed, less tangible, less susceptible to definition. One cannot embrace a wild, untamed force like neo-liberal globalisation, even in a modified form, and expect it to be otherwise. The values of a liberal society – beyond its institutional axioms – are difficult to express in concrete terms at the best of times because they encompass so much diversity and contradiction. The values of artists regularly challenge those of the political elite; the values of environmentalists have often been at odds with those of business people; the values of progressives have usually contradicted those of conservatives. But in an age of globalised information flow, rapid and frequent human travel and global commerce, people's value systems and identities are less geographically bound than at any other time in human history. The emergence of global environmentalist movements, of global (rather than national) Islamist identity movements, including terrorist groups, and of global entrepreneurs prepared to change their citizenship as the commercial need arises – all these are merely symptoms of this process. There are more "citizens of the world" than ever. Of course, the opposite phenomenon of heightened parochialism is also at work. Libertarians in Texas are rejecting their American identity and campaigning to secede from the union. Scottish calls for secession from Britain are getting louder and stronger, to the point where the *Daily Telegraph* in London saw fit to run a wonderfully blunt "Call Yourself British" campaign. But this only reinforces the point that everywhere, identity and culture are becoming radically heterogenous.

Neo-conservatives simply ignore these irreversible trends. They posit a clear, identifiable, unproblematic national culture; a culture that was comparatively homogenous until the relativism of the Left tore at its fabric. This is an ossified, nostalgic fiction. It is not merely descriptive. It is ideologically active in its own right. The history on which this nostalgia is based is also ideologically coloured. So the diggers in Gallipoli were fighting for freedom (rather than the British Empire), just as those in Iraq were fighting for freedom. Or similarly, ours is a culture that stems from the Judeo-Christian tradition, in spite of the fact that the Jewish tradition is very different from the Christian one, and very many Christians before World War II would probably have been repulsed at the connection being drawn. These are new constructions, presented as history for the purpose of creating what masquerades as an old, established culture. Neo-conservative monoculturalism therefore does not truly protect a current state of being, or even an old one. It wishes away the chaotic order that has prevailed, and that neo-liberalism has, in no small part, unleashed. It is, to borrow from Ludwig Wittgenstein, attempting to repair a broken spider web with bare hands. The grand irony is that by taking up neo-liberalism, conservatism became the very thing Hayek once (incorrectly in my view) derided it for being:

> Like the socialist, [the conservative] is less concerned with the problem of how the powers of government should be limited than with that of who wields them; and, like the socialist, he regards himself as entitled to force the value he holds on other people.

When I say that the conservative lacks principles, I do not mean to suggest that he lacks moral conviction. The typical conservative is indeed usually a man of very strong moral convictions. What I mean is that he has no political principles which enable him to work with people whose moral values differ from his own for a political order in which both can obey their convictions. It is the recognition of such principles that permits the coexistence of different sets of values that makes it possible to build a peaceful society with a minimum of force. The acceptance of such principles means that we agree to tolerate much that we dislike ...

To the liberal neither moral nor religious ideals are proper objects of coercion, while both conservatives and socialists recognize no such limits. I sometimes feel that the most conspicuous attribute of liberalism that distinguishes it as much from conservatism as from socialism is the view that moral beliefs concerning matters of conduct which do not directly interfere with the protected sphere of other persons do not justify coercion. This may also explain why it seems to be so much easier for the repentant socialist to find a new spiritual home in the conservative fold than in the liberal.

If we replace "conservative" with "neo-conservative" in this passage, it has a remarkable ring of truth – right down to its appeal among former socialists.

Often, this kind of cultural politics is described as "social conservatism." To the extent that its tensions with neo-liberal economics are acknowledged at all, it is presented as a kind of "balance"; one that militates against the market's social upheaval. John Howard put it the following way:

People want a bit of constancy in their lives. If you've got a lot of rapid economic change, you want a bit of anchorage in ordinary life. The one, in a sense, reinforces and complements the other. The key to our success in office was that we did, generally speaking,

govern according to the principles of liberalism in economic policy
and with a fairly conservative social agenda, which I not only
believed in but was also appropriate for the times.

Howard is undoubtedly correct that this was electorally effective. But
to present it as a matter of complementary approaches is philosophically
misleading. It is not a matter of "balance"; it is a matter of contradiction.
And partly for this reason, there is little about this cultural politics that is
truly conservative. Indeed, it behaves in ways that violate the best insights
of conservatism.

A conservative understands that lecturing migrants on adopting a new
culture is a futile exercise because she or he knows that cultural commitments are not simply commodities from which one makes an unbounded
choice. The individual, migrant or otherwise, is partly a product of a
social and cultural history that they cannot simply shed, for better or
worse. Conservatism accepts this as part of its politics of imperfection, in
the knowledge that ignoring the complexities and frailties of human
nature is likely only to make things worse. Cultural commitments evolve,
and for most individuals integration with their environment is a natural
and gradual process. That implies that individuals should be more or less
left to their own devices. Assimilation – an inorganic, top-down approach
to culture – is an emphatically progressive project, not a conservative one.
Conservatism tells us it is likely only to be counter-productive and to promote hostile and reactionary counter-cultures.

It is possible, as I have said earier, that a conservative may legitimately
wish to restrict migration on the basis that the rapid proliferation of
diverse cultural values would cause uncomfortably rapid social change. But
this very argument acknowledges the fact that the cultural constitutions of
individuals do not simply change at will. The conservative would certainly
not run immigration at record levels for economic reasons (as the Howard
government did) and then lecture its migrant population on what their
values should be. That is especially true where this is done pursuant to a

neo-liberal plan, where individuals are encouraged to use their mobility for entrepreneurial reasons, not cultural ones. The conservative takes the world as it is, not as she or he wishes it to be. And it is a world in which pluralisms in culture, politics and identity within a society are an inescapable and irreversible fact of life.

Certainly, pluralism has its limits, which is why the foundational institutions of our society remain vital. The rule of law must be upheld; the courts must remain independent; the political system must preserve its integrity. But none of these institutions is enhanced by telling citizens what their values should be. If conservatives seek to salvage a common culture, it should be done by the State expressing those values in its own conduct. So, for instance, conservative parties should refuse funds from violent, sexist or racist organisations if they believe these are important values to preserve. When in government they should not fund organisations or initiatives that violate these ideas. And, most problematically for neo-liberals, they should be prepared to limit the market's operation when it violates these values. That would ultimately be more effective and more philosophically consistent than the kind of neo-conservative culture warring that has prevailed. Neo-conservatism's marriage with neo-liberalism, however, makes this impossible because it takes defence of a largely unfettered free market as its starting point. This leaves it very little option other than to shout its cultural orthodoxy at people. This is quintessentially reactionary.

Of course, no one can deny that this approach is politically profitable — at least in the short term. No doubt it has its effect among key constituencies in the electorate. It is a well-rehearsed theme in Australian electoral analysis that the Howard government's cultural politics were devastatingly successful in stealing Labor's blue-collar base for the Coalition. It is true that "Howard's battlers" were alienated by Keating's progressive cultural program, and that many of them found succour in the nostalgic and xenophobic parochialism of Pauline Hanson. It is also true that One Nation's emergence did considerable electoral damage to the Coalition in 1998, and that Howard was politically ingenious in adopting chunks of Hanson's narrative to turn the tide. But this essay is not concerned with the game of politics. It is concerned with its animating philosophies, especially as they relate to liberalism and conservatism. In the long term, ideas matter more than party politics.

Of course, the Howard era has now come to an end, which raises its own questions about the future direction of conservative politics in Australia. The answer to those questions depends very much on whether Australian neo-conservatism was ultimately a phenomenon of John Howard, or whether it represented a deeper philosophical shift, of which Howard was only the figurehead. This soon after Howard's defeat there is clearly insufficient empirical evidence on which to judge definitively. The Liberal Party's spectacular internal pyrotechnics since 2007 suggest that it is a live debate that is yet to run its course.

Signs of neo-conservative continuity remain, particularly in the form of Kevin Andrews. Andrews, you will recall, was the Howard immigration minister who utterly politicised the law-enforcement and judicial process surrounding Dr Mohammed Haneef, who was so farcically charged with terrorism offences. Such a brutalising of our institutions of justice is the very opposite of conservative, but it does fit neatly with the neo-conservative pattern of cultural politics. That much became clear when, on the eve of the 2007 election, Andrews announced he would cut African immigration because Sudanese migrants were not integrating sufficiently. Incredibly, the event that inspired this was the murder of Liep Gony, an eighteen-year-old Sudanese refugee, by two white kids. The culture of these assailants and their capacity to integrate, of course, was not questioned: only those of the victim. At the time it seemed a desperate political attempt from a sinking government, and perhaps it was. But it seems to reflect Andrews' continuing convictions. As recently as October 2009, he was again spruiking for a debate on "Muslim enclaves" and blaming "political correctness" – a result of that leftist orthodoxy – for the fact that the issue had not been ventilated as he would have liked.

Andrews' Liberal colleague Greg Hunt immediately distanced himself, affirming only that Australia's "approach should be colour-blind, ethnicity-blind, background-blind, but simply focused on [migrants'] ability to contribute." Andrews' approach is also at odds with the kind of social commentary to have emerged within the Liberal Party in the past year that was conspicuously absent during the Howard era. Here, for instance, is Christopher Pyne on ABC television's *Q&A*, talking about fellow panellist Sabrina Houssami, a Muslim woman and former Miss World Australia:

> I worry that the reason why Sabrina is, you know, seen to be part of the community is because Sabrina looks very much like the rest of the community, and so therefore she is a role model. But we shouldn't regard Sabrina as different to somebody who is in full purda. The person in full purda is a human being who deserves full respect as well …
>
> I just think there's a danger in the media saying, "Let's put Sabrina up there because Sabrina looks like us, so therefore, you know, she's a good role model." But she's a human being, the person who is in full *purda* is a human being, the Aboriginals who live amongst us in the city, who work amongst us with coats and ties – you know, people say, you know, "These are good role models," but the person who lives a tribal lifestyle in Central Australia, they're a human being too, they should all be treated exactly the same way.

The shadow treasurer, Joe Hockey, echoed these sentiments in November in an address to the Sydney Institute:

> We must accept the right of people to follow whatever religion they choose, to wear what they want and undertake their own rituals of observance. It always perplexes me that so many people worry about Muslim women wearing the hijab when for centuries and even in some places today, Catholic nuns dress in similar attire.

What is important is that the practitioners of any faith respect the rights of others and the freedom of every individual to determine their own faith. Yes, we should condemn those governments that force women to cover themselves from head to toe whether it is their choice or not. But we should not concern ourselves with people who make those choices themselves, as many Muslim women do.

And in a similarly liberal vein, though on a broader theme, here is the then opposition leader, Malcolm Turnbull, also on *Q&A*:

If I could make one practical suggestion which I've seen in schools in my own area, where you do have a large group of students from one country or one part of the world – you know, they might be Russian, for example – one really good thing is to have a Russian language program or it could be a language program from the refugee group in your school that all of the children get invited to participate in so that there is a sort of a sharing of the cultural experiences from both groups, because I think one of the great – I think our greatest strength as a nation is our diversity and I think our cultural curiosity is enormously important and so what we should be encouraging is not just saying to refugees or immigrants generally, "You have got to become part of – you've got to sort of learn the way we do things." We should be reaching out and learning more about your culture, because the truth is our diversity and the fact that we have so many cultural backgrounds is one of our greatest strengths.

It is now a matter of historical record that Kevin Andrews was a key figure in undermining the leadership of Malcolm Turnbull, which finally met its death in December 2009. The key issue, of course, was not multiculturalism, social cohesion or indeed any other theme of cultural politics. It was climate change, and specifically Turnbull's support for an amended form of Labor's emissions trading scheme (ETS). Presently, when looking for clues as to the future direction of conservative politics in Australia, this issue seems the most instructive place to look. It is to the current political moment what culture and national security were to the previous one. The global financial crisis is naturally a contender in this regard, and certainly it raises momentous philosophical questions for the neo-liberal neo-conservative alliance. But climate change promises to be a more ongoing political conundrum that will be of lasting philosophical consequence. For this reason, and also because it has so clearly driven a wedge through conservative politics in this country, it seems to be the perfect lens through which to discern the current and future state of Australian conservatism.

A FIGHT TO THE POLITICAL DEATH

At first blush, climate change might seem to be the kind of issue that is ideologically neutral. It is, after all, a matter of scientific determination, not political persuasion. It is not about theories of human society, but observation of natural phenomena. That, of course, is a misleading portrait. As it happens, climate change is the most ideologically charged issue we are likely to witness for generations.

Let us admit up-front the most obvious, but resolutely denied, fact of the climate change debate. It is not, for many of its participants, about science at all. That goes for those who want action as much as those who deny climate change exists. Unless we are ourselves climatologists, the truth, if we're being honest with ourselves, is that none of us really has any idea about climate science. We are unlikely to have pored over the refereed journals where the scientific debates take place. Even if we have, we are very unlikely to have been able to understand them. We might cite statistics, and the conclusions of scientific reports, but we lack the intellectual tools to evaluate them. For those who accept climate change as a real and present danger that demands political action, this is not much of a problem. The overwhelming weight of information available to the public suggests that a very large majority of climate scientists are so convinced of the reality and danger of climate change that they are now more concerned with how bad the problem is, than whether it exists. True, that information is filtered through media – as most public information is – but climate believers are prepared to accept what appears to be the conventional wisdom among those best placed to know. They cannot honestly claim to know the veracity of climate change for themselves, but they are happy to delegate this task to climate scientists, and to rely on the media to transmit their findings. In this way, there is a clear parallel with the scientific consensus on the theory of evolution. Most people cannot honestly claim sufficient scientific knowledge to adjudicate on the issue independently, but since almost every scientist seems to subscribe to the theory, they accept it.

There is nothing particularly unusual about this. In fact, we take this approach to most issues in life of which we do not have direct knowledge. Most of us do not, for instance, have any way to measure inflation or unemployment – we rely instead on economists to measure these things and tell us. Then, we almost never read their reports, instead placing our trust in media reports that give us the figures. Without delegating this sort of information-gathering, we would simply be unable to live our lives.

For those who deny climate change (or describe themselves as "sceptics"), problems arise. The overwhelming scientific consensus projected through mass media means they have two choices if they wish to maintain their denial: 1) they can find a scientist they consider to be authoritative who espouses their view; or 2) they can attempt to engage directly with the science and make their own judgment. Often they do both, appealing to the authority of a particular scientist and attempting to argue their case from the scientific data directly. The first approach, at least, is a more honest one. The second is comically dishonest. Few things are more absurd to witness than a blogger, journalist or pundit who is not a scientist attempting to make the scientific argument against climate change. The very endeavour is deceitful because it represents to the world that the denier has the scientific skills necessary to interpret the data, when this is almost certainly not true. Science is not simply the production of data. It is the discipline of being able to discern which data are relevant, which data are reliable, and then of knowing how to interpret them. These are not skills available to just any internet junkie.

The option of appealing to the authority of a scientist who denies climate change may be more honest, but it raises conundrums of its own. Why accept the word of a scientist who appears to be in a very small minority? Certainly, it is possible for a majority of scientists to be wrong, and for a minority to triumph in the long run, but on what basis can the layman be confident that that is true in this case? Here again, the climate-change denier has two options: 1) to argue that the relevant scientist is in fact not in the minority – or at least not a small one; or 2) to argue that the majority of scientists are in fact lying. Either view is almost inevitably conspiratorial. The first argument implies that the media have (probably deliberately) misled their audiences as to the true state of scientific opinion, and that all the scientists given the task of assessing the issue for governments around the world as well as the United Nations are chosen because they comply with climate-change orthodoxy. The second argument raises an obvious question: why would these scientists be lying? Presumably it is because they are ideologically driven or they derive some other benefit from lying. Perhaps they are being bribed, or they are seeking the favour of people in power. Either way, this argument rests on a conspiracy theory that climate change is an ideological construction.

That sort of view echoes very closely the neo-conservative idea of a "new class": the leftist elite identified by Irving Kristol that is after the power to remake our civilisation. Scientists, you will recall, were among this new class. It is therefore entirely plausible within this worldview that they would approach their scientific work with the ideological ambition of increasing the size of government and imposing their orthodoxy on the world. The science of climate change fits the bill perfectly: it implies an increased role for government that must intervene in the workings of the market to limit environmental damage.

Of course, it is possible that climate-change activists are motivated more by their ideological commitments than by their trust in the scientific consensus. It is conceivable that staunch opponents of capitalism may leap on the opportunity climate change provides to argue for the destruction of the market's political dominance. But it is also conceivable – and probably much more common – for climate-change believers to take their position based on trust in what they perceive to be conventional wisdom. Climate-change denialism on the part of non-scientists, by contrast, is always an ideological or an emotional process. The intellectual lengths required to sustain it are only feasible for those who have pre-existing reasons for *wanting* to deny it. That may be because its implications are devastating for one's present livelihood – as might presently be true of certain farmers, or people working in high-emissions industries – in which case the response is probably emotional. Or it might be because it counters one's deeply held views of the world, in which case the response is ideological. Here again we have an echo with anti-evolutionism, which is often the position of non-scientists who see evolution as a threat to their religious convictions. In each case, it is a result-orientated approach to the issue. It begins with the position (denying the apparent scientific consensus), and then looks for ways of supporting it.

This is crucial to understand in making sense of conservative and neo-conservative responses to climate change. Neo-conservative politics is far more compatible with climate-change denial than with its acceptance. Denial quenches the neo-conservative thirst for an enemy elite, dividing the world once more into friends and enemies, and turning the discussion into an ideological contest. But most importantly, it allows neo-conservatives to retain their ideological fidelity to neo-liberalism, concealing the fundamental contradiction between the two things. The simple fact is that neo-liberalism is incompatible with the politics of climate-change response. In order for neo-liberalism to be preserved, climate change must, in the first instance, be denied.

The reasons for this are easily deducible from the central neo-liberal idea that the market is not simply a means for generating and distributing wealth in society: it is a social and political rationality. As noted above, this implies that the market itself is the arbiter of political value, and that accordingly its consequences cannot be deemed unjust or negative in any meaningful sense. Hayek himself noted fleetingly the possibility of environmental degradation from the operation of the market, but apparently considered it unimportant. It is this sort of thinking that drove Reagan's decision to cut the funding of the Environmental Protection Agency and reject that agency's proposals to counter the environmental concern of the day, acid rain. Reagan simply thought acid rain was unimportant, and saw this environmental agenda as an additional restraint on industry. And in the kind of neo-liberal and neo-conservative fashion that is now extremely familiar, Reagan doubted the scientific evidence that suggested acid rain was caused by pollution from American industry. It is noteworthy that Reagan's attitude towards ozone-layer depletion was more environmentally active, but then the economics were very different, too. American companies were further advanced in developing alternatives to CFCs than their European competitors, and so they stood to benefit handsomely from a global agreement to reduce CFC production. In each case, the decision appears not to have been made on environmental grounds.

The problem for neo-liberalism is that climate change, as articulated by the scientists that warn us about it, is so self-evidently catastrophic that it simply cannot be dismissed as unimportant. Similarly, if its ultimate cause is carbon emissions – overwhelmingly from untrammelled industry – then it becomes impossible to sustain the neo-liberal position that the market's consequences should simply be accepted rather than regulated. The rendering uninhabitable of much of the planet just cannot be theorised away in this manner. That leaves neo-liberals with only the option of denial. That denial takes two main forms. The first is outright denial of climate change as a phenomenon, where arguments are put that the planet is actually cooling rather than warming, contrary to what climate-change orthodoxy tells us. The second form of denial accepts that climate change is occurring but argues that it is simply the natural process of climate variability that we have seen throughout the planet's history, and that – most importantly – it is not the result of human activity. The market is thereby exonerated, and neo-liberalism can remain intact.

There is much at stake here. Climate change presents more than a political challenge for neo-liberalism; it threatens to invalidate it. In this respect it is an even greater threat than the global financial crisis, because it is still open to neo-liberals to claim that the problem in that case was that neo-liberalism was not applied with sufficient rigour. That is a less plausible argument on climate change. The battle over the truth of climate-change science is therefore a political fight to the death for neo-liberalism.

In ideological terms it is similar to the Cold War, with one important exception: there is no clear, distinct and unified ideological opponent akin to communism.

That is where neo-conservatism becomes so important to climate denialism. It constructs the ideological foe that is needed to sustain the fight. Against this background, it is wholly unsurprising to recall Senator Nick Minchin's deeply ideological take on the issue:

> For the extreme Left it provides the opportunity to do what they've always wanted to do, to sort of de-industrialise the Western world. You know the collapse of communism was a disaster for the Left, and the, and really they embraced environmentalism as their new religion.

A clearer expression of the neo-liberal neo-conservative faith is difficult to find. Climate change is basically a conspiracy of the "new class." It is the continuation of communism by other means, the reignition of the Cold War. The natural consequence for Minchin – one of the Liberal Party's most neo-liberal members – is that he *cannot* accept the reality of climate change without losing the ideological war he has constructed. Environmentalism simply must be the fringe ideology of the Cold War's vanquished combatants. Any chance that the environment might become a mainstream issue – particularly where it suggests the curtailment of capitalism – shakes the very foundation of Minchin's worldview. Minchin is not alone in his dystopian vision. On his recent tour of Australia, the celebrity sceptic and former Thatcher advisor Lord Christopher Monckton played to a similar theme, warning that accepting climate change would place us at the mercy of

> a huge army of new bureaucracies to enforce the will of those whom you do not elect on those whom you do. And this is what they were going to be given the power to do: to take control over all formerly free markets and set the market rules. So control or to rig the market.

By the time Monckton had described climate-change protesters at Copenhagen as "Hitler Youth," it had become clear that this was not a matter of the life and death of the planet. For such ideologues, it is much more important than that.

This helps explain why it is that a person's position on climate change can be predicted with quite remarkable accuracy from the seemingly unrelated matter of their social politics. I cannot claim to have surveyed the Australian commentariat comprehensively, but I cannot immediately think of a single columnist or broadcaster who spruiked Howard's neo-conservative cultural politics and who is not also a climate-change denier or sceptic. If such a person exists, he or she is certainly in a very small minority. A brief survey of the Liberal Party politicians so angered by the ETS includes a striking number of those with something approximating neo-conservative cultural politics: Kevin Andrews, Eric Abetz, Sophie Mirabella, Cory Bernardi, Bronwyn Bishop, Nick Minchin, Tony Abbott (though Abbott is a more complex character than the others), Wilson Tuckey (though he is always a unique case) and before the latest show-down, Brendan Nelson. By contrast, the ETS-friendly Liberals seem over-whelmingly to be those whose cultural politics differ from those of Howard: Malcolm Turnbull, Christopher Pyne, Joe Hockey, Judith Troeth, George Brandis, Greg Hunt. John Howard himself did finally propose an ETS before the 2007 election, but it was a hasty concoction. He had held out on any action on climate change and tried to boost the sceptics' case for as long as possible until he saw the political inevitability. The correlation, even if not necessarily complete, is certainly strong enough to suggest there is an ideological continuity at work here.

The split is truly remarkable when one considers exactly what the proposed ETS was. It was scarcely a green manifesto, and indeed was clearly vulnerable to attack on environmental grounds. It gave large wads of compensation to the nation's biggest polluters, and was tied to modest emissions reduction targets – less than those demanded by the scientific orthodoxy. Most fundamentally, though, it was a market-based solution to the problem. In this respect it is about as close as neo-liberalism can get to mustering a response. Indeed, it is a testament to the ideological dominance of neo-liberalism that this is the approach the Labor government favoured. There are several other ways one might choose to respond to climate change. The simplest, and probably most effective, would be to introduce a carbon tax. An approach that gives radical priority to the environment over industry would use regulation to make certain levels of emission illegal. Only someone in debt to the logic of neo-liberalism would conceive of responding by creating a new market, this time in what are essentially pollution permits. It provides entrepreneurs with the chance to make money from climate-change policy in a way that neither a carbon tax nor regulation does. It also keeps intact the narrative of a market society. If ever a climate-change response was going to be acceptable to a neo-liberal, this was it.

Moreover, it had been negotiated under Turnbull to reduce the economic shock its implementation might have. This gave it some important conservative credentials. With polling consistently showing that a significant majority of the electorate wants action on climate change, and with international politics stumbling ineptly towards some kind of action, it could well be argued that some kind of climate-change policy, at least in Australia, is inevitable. The political implications were clear enough for Malcolm Turnbull to declare that a Coalition without a climate-change policy would be wiped out at the next election. Even the new Liberal Party leadership, built on the support of climate-change denialists and sceptics, seems tacitly to have accepted that assessment, with Tony Abbott pledging immediately on taking the leadership that the Liberal Party would develop an effective policy, but that it would not be an ETS or a new tax. Given these facts on the ground, it is entirely open to a conservative to adopt Arthur Balfour's pragmatic dictum that there is "no point in resisting what [is] bound to come." The role of the conservative, then, would be to minimise the impact of the change. Surely that is precisely what Turnbull had attempted to do by negotiating an ETS with the Labor government that enraged environmentalists but reduced the economic disruption inherent in Labor's original bill.

The result has been perverse. Initially we had the spectacle of Tony Abbott considering a climate-change response through regulation. This is probably the most radical option for tackling climate change that exists. It is the kind of thing a progressive does. It is certainly not neo-liberal, although Abbott has long established his neo-liberal credentials and quickly found himself talking up the prospect of reintroducing elements of Work-Choices. Then, upon the resumption of parliament, Abbott's Coalition released a climate-change policy that permits industry to continue with "business as usual" without any increased costs at all. Detail is scant, but it seems the policy is tied not to emissions but to what Abbott has called "emissions intensity." The difference is crucial. "Emissions" denotes an environmental concept concerned with absolute environmental impact. "Emissions intensity" is an economic concept that considers the rate of emissions against productivity. Accordingly, emissions may continue to rise while emissions intensity remains constant. The Coalition's policy, then, could see an increase in emissions without consequence, provided those increased emissions occur in line with "business as usual." Only where polluters increase their emissions intensity will they be penalised, and to date there is no detail on how severe those penalties would be – or even if they would outweigh the increased profits pollution might bring. We know only that these penalties will be set in consultation with industry and that they are "only expected to apply in exceptional circumstances."

That all sounds resoundingly neo-liberal because it makes sacred the market's "business as usual" operations. But consider that under this policy, industry may also apply for grants from an Emissions Reduction Fund for projects that reduce emissions. Here it is the State that becomes the arbiter of which projects get funded, and (presumably) it is the taxpayer who funds it. On this point, the Coalition's policy is one of central planning. Abbott has managed to conjure a policy that, depending on which aspect one considers, is both more and less neo-liberal than an ETS, which is to say it is philosophically inconsistent. It is difficult to know what to make of this in assessing the implications for conservatism's future direction, or indeed whether we should take it seriously enough to analyse it in ideological terms at all. Abbott's own position on climate change seems to be one of high scepticism, and probably denial. His policy appears to be a gesture to those in his party and the electorate who are demanding some sort of action, but one which does not offend the denialists that make up his support base. Asked why he would propose a solution for a problem that he does not believe exists, Abbott responded by saying he did not wish to impose his view of the issue on the entire nation: that is, this is an exercise in symbolic politics on the basis that Abbott recognises the need to be seen to be doing something. At this point Abbott's divergent messages seem merely to express the state of ideological confusion in which the Liberal Party presently finds itself.

TH∃ FUTURE OF CONSERVATISM

The decades spanning the late twentieth and early twenty-first centuries were a wonderful time to be a neo-conservative. The cultural fracture inherent in neo-liberalism ensured that its strong, assured, dogmatic (even if philosophically inconsistent) cultural politics would resonate among its audience. The advent of global terrorism against Western nations only strengthened the emotional pull of this cultural discourse and, as terrorism tends to do, tilted the political terrain in favour of aggression and ideological belligerence. Neo-conservatism, perhaps due to its influences from progressive political traditions such as Marxism and Trotskyism, thrives in this sort of environment. Everyone is looking for an enemy at such times, and neo-conservatism provides them with clarity, and in abundance.

Things changed around 2007. The issues that had dominated politics in the English-speaking world – terrorism, the war in Iraq, the culture wars – began to lose their urgency and political purchase. Moreover, neo-conservative policies in these areas seemed manifestly to have failed: the Iraq war was a debacle, and the War on Terror became symbolised by the scandalous revelations coming out of Guantánamo Bay. The Bush administration had become putridly unpopular, tarnishing the popular acceptance of the War on Terror with it. Politics suddenly entered a post-terror phase. In Britain, Prime Minister Gordon Brown attempted to introduce tougher new anti-terrorism laws, only to be accused – by conservative politicians and newspapers – of trying to exploit terrorism for cynical political gain. In the United States, a candidate with no compelling foreign policy credentials, Barack Obama, defeated a former war hero, John McCain, to claim the presidency. That, of course, followed the Australian election that saw John Howard lose government and his own seat as Kevin Rudd swept to power. The issues that defined that campaign were extremely uncomfortable ones for neo-liberal neo-conservatives, most notably industrial relations and climate change.

The fall for conservative parties in the Anglosphere has been as steep as the rise. Australia's Coalition is presently in disarray. The Republicans in the United States are in the minority in both houses of Congress and it is very difficult to identify who their next president could be. The financial crisis has hit the spiritual home of neo-liberalism particularly hard, and created considerable ideological problems for Republican renewal. The Republicans have been captured by their most radical, presently unelectable neo-conservative fringe: shock-jock Rush Limbaugh is their unofficial spokesman, Dick Cheney the loudest voice on foreign affairs, and Sarah Palin the rising star. In Britain, the Tories have already been out of power for twelve years. It is true that they will almost certainly remove Labour from government in this year's election, but their leader, David Cameron, is sounding decidedly different from a neo-liberal, standing up at Davos and talking about things like "capitalism with a conscience" and the rejection of the "old economic orthodoxy." He has weighed in vigorously on the "sexualisation and excessive commercialisation" of young people and warned businesses and advertisers that if they continue in such a manner, he might introduce legislation to stop it. He has also appointed a trade union envoy and offered to address the Trades Union Congress. A cartoon in the *Guardian* captures the point, depicting Cameron declaring, "The Tory's tie is deepest red, who says that socialism's dead?"

In this essay, I have argued that by embracing neo-liberalism, conservatives have backed themselves into an ideological corner that has forced them to violate the philosophical tenets of both liberalism and conservatism and to adopt a thoroughly reactionary form of politics. The question now is whether or not the liberal conservative tradition is salvageable, and if it is, what it might look like in a world radically and irreversibly changed from the one that gave birth to it. These are questions of the utmost importance because the liberal and conservative traditions contain indispensable wisdom for the functioning of our politics. A political culture deprived of their vibrant presence, particularly where it has known them for so long, is a deeply impoverished one.

I must confess that I am not optimistic. Ours is a world that has changed irrevocably. The revolutionary consequences of neo-liberalism cannot simply be unwound by returning to some real or imagined past. This new social environment is one where political borders mean less than they once did, and where the thought of organic social homogeneity is merely a nostalgic fantasy. If there is to be homogeneity, then it must be forced, which is both un-conservative and illiberal. Contrary to the dreams of neo-liberalism, we are not heading towards a world unified by a global market culture. Indeed, we are not in the midst of some transition to a global culture of any kind. There is, and there will be, no "global community" except in the artificial sense that we use when we refer collectively to the nation-states of the world. We are witnessing the logical consequence of neo-liberalism in practice: the wild proliferation of new cultural and social forms, as well as new identities – some parochial, some globalist, some radically individualist, some profoundly collectivist. Of course, diversity has always existed in human society, but it was regulated in an informal way by the historical continuities and social norms that lent societies a level of coherence.

The much-mourned breakdown of community and of family has been accompanied by the corresponding emergence of new forms of these. Today's most vibrant communities seem to be virtual and de-territorialised (though not necessarily socially rich), and the traditional nuclear family is merely one (by no means dominant) feature of the social landscape. Combined with mass migration and the globalisation of information, this means that the historical continuities and social norms that matter to people have very little to do with their geography now, and far more to do with their identity. The most attention-grabbing example of this in recent years has been the emergence of home-grown Islamist terrorism, where identity, ethnicity and geography are radically separated in a way that was not possible until quite recently. Our social world – and this is especially true for diverse, young nations such as Australia and the United States – is one that is inevitably made up of innumerable value systems, histories and cultural memories that must coexist rather than compete for dominance. This is dynamic, at times exhilarating, but also revolutionary. No amount of cultural orthodoxy from politicians can alter it. Conservatives have every right to lament these developments, but in the best traditions of conservatism, they should accept their irreversible reality. The alternative is to make conservatism reactionary and obsolete as a coherent philosophy.

An implication of this is that liberalism and conservatism will have their best chance of thriving through the disavowal of neo-liberalism. If that is to happen, the time is now. The political logic of climate change and the global financial crisis suggest that an ideological retreat would not only be philosophically coherent, but politically fashionable. The common thread connecting these political issues is a widely held view that the untamed operations of the market were a major contributing factor in the creation of such problems. The short-term goals of profit that prevail in the marketplace have thus far proven incompatible with the long-term challenges of conserving the environment, and the long-term desirability of fostering economic (and with it, social) stability.

If the conservative link with neo-liberalism can be severed, this will free conservatives to accept and then confront the biggest political issues of the day, including climate change. At present, the most ardent neo-liberal neo-conservatives are gambling their ideological future on winning the debate about the climate-change hoax. This is not only deeply ideological, it is highly risky. If they lose that debate, as seems likely, they will have dealt themselves out of the political discourse altogether. A renewed liberal conservative tradition must treat environmental concerns with the utmost seriousness and demonstrate strong environmental credentials. In philosophical terms, that should be easy enough to do – not just on the basis that environmental protection is a prudent form of risk management, but on the basis that conservation is a fundamentally conservative value. It is the ideologies of progress that should constitute the most serious threat to the environment because they are more inclined to sweep aside any environmental barriers to their progressive goals. This is precisely what neo-liberalism has ended up doing, mainly because it is such a progressive ideology.

That does *not* mean – and this is crucial – that any renewed liberal conservatism should countenance doing away with the market. The market has proven itself to be an invaluable institution in the West and elsewhere. Moreover, it is an indispensable ally in confronting environmental challenges such as global warming. As John Gray has observed in making the case for a green conservatism, the lesson of modern political history is that the greatest environmental devastation is caused not by market actors, but by central planning. He cites the example of the Soviet Union, a fifth of which became an ecological disaster area, and another 30–40 per cent of which were places of ecological stress. Air pollution reached astronomical levels, causing occasionally drastic reductions in life expectancy. In Gray's view, events such as the Chernobyl disaster were neither isolated incidents (he lists several others) nor freakish anomalies. Rather, they were characteristic of the political system, which was geared to the Soviet aim of unrestricted economic development through a centrally planned model. The key lesson is that "the destruction of the environment proceeds most swiftly, and often most irreversibly, in a state of nature lacking in law and property rights." Where all land is held in common, it becomes susceptible to overuse and depletion. Private property gives people an interest in using land sustainably so that it continues to have value. Similarly, conservatives will accept that market institutions and market imperatives should be harnessed in the aid of environmental sustainability, possibly through the development of new, green technologies. That idea is now a mainstream one, but it is not open to ideologues still obsessed with proving a climate-change conspiracy.

But the market is not infallible, and it must be subordinated to political restraint. It is a valuable institution if used in the service of society, but a horribly destructive one when elevated to the level of a supreme rationality: a wonderful servant, but a dangerous master. Conservatives should intuit this and be prepared to curtail its operation where necessary in the interests of environmental sustainability or social integrity. Obviously, that is easier to state as a matter of principle than to apply – after all, there is bound to be disagreement on what constitutes anti-social market behaviour. Indeed, those disagreements are only likely to multiply in a time of radical and increasing pluralism. I accept these ambiguities present themselves, but the broad principle is still important because it implies a rejection of the axioms of neo-liberal discourse, where the presence of an economic cost is often deemed sufficient reason to dismiss a policy. This alternative approach implies that politics becomes less concerned with the goal of perpetual economic growth, and more with economic and social stability.

If that seems regressive, it is because our politics has become so beholden to progressivism. Conservatism should be naturally comfortable with a different approach that recognises the unsustainability of our present economic practices. Few should understand better than conservatives that much of our world is characterised by trade-offs. We cannot grow an economy perpetually because the environment imposes natural limits on us. Surely, at this moment in history when the global economy has revealed its fragility and the environment is revealing the limits of its capacity, conservatism must return to its philosophical starting point and shun the dream of progress for its own sake. The world now needs conservatives to do what they have always done best: to identify and respect limits, not to pursue some utopian fantasy that we can expand them indefinitely. That is a fantasy Homo economicus will be loath to renounce, but it is one that conservatism, shorn of neo-liberal attachments, is well equipped to forego.

In the social and cultural realm, some conservative pragmatism is in order. Our society has changed enormously and its diversity will only multiply. The task of conservatism is not to remake the social world in accordance with a nostalgic order. It is to find a way to reconcile people with these new circumstances. In that sense, despite the legitimate liberal arguments against multiculturalism, it is a policy that is now best embraced by liberal conservatives. It was, after all, conservatives who introduced the policy here, and polling has consistently shown that very large majorities of the Australian people support it. In this regard, and despite its pretensions to speak for the "mainstream," neo-conservative anti-multiculturalism lags behind the dominant public attitude. The public has already reconciled itself with multicultural policy, and there is little reason other than ideological dogma to attempt to fracture that reconciliation. Given that multiculturalism has become an established feature of Australian society, it is almost impossible to try to remove it without a whiff of nostalgia and xenophobia. Although an anti-multicultural discourse almost certainly proceeds in the name of social cohesion and unity, its effect on a diverse population already satisfied with multiculturalism will only be division, the inflammation of social tensions, and the kinds of identity politics that stem from exclusion. New ways of forging social unity must be found.

Naturally, conservatives will be, and should be, resolutely opposed to pure cultural or moral relativism, but here too they should be honest enough to recognise that Australian multiculturalism has never meant this, and that nothing of the sort currently prevails in Australia's institutions. Honour killings are not, and never will be, legally tolerated. Sexual and racial discrimination laws have been in place for over three decades and show no sign of disappearing. With the exception of the right of religious institutions to discriminate on religious grounds (a right that has little to do with migrant demands), neither culture nor religion is a defence before the law.

For multiculturalism to be liberal, though, it should be rooted in individual rights to cultural self-determination. Happily for liberal conservatives, it always has been, as Geoffrey Brahm Levey observed in the *Griffith Review*:

> Australian multicultural policy is highly individualistic ... It is each
> individual who enjoys the rights (such as those to cultural identity

and respect, and access to equity) and bears the responsibilities (of abiding by Australia's liberal-democratic institutions) under the policy. Lest there be any ambiguity, the National Agenda goes on to state that: "Fundamentally, multiculturalism is about the rights of the individual."

That leaves open the question of national identity. In an age of remarkable and increasing social fluidity, this is a difficult question for conservatives to approach in any coherent way. Any attempt to define national identity with reference to a narrowly defined history and culture is likely not to be sufficiently compelling to a diverse nation. The challenge globalisation throws up is to articulate national identities that are broad and inclusive in a way that they have often not previously needed to be. That does not mean they must amount to nothing, just that they must amount to something with broad resonance.

In this respect, liberal conservatism may be well served by returning to its liberal roots. I have argued elsewhere that this is the secret to America's resilient and pervasive sense of patriotism and national identity under globalised conditions. In this respect it is notably different from European nations, which attract very little fidelity from their minority communities. The difference is not, as many neo-conservatives claim, that Europe's flirtation with multiculturalism has killed its sense of self and allowed its recalcitrant minorities to disappear into a fog of cultural relativism and escape any sense of loyalty to the nation. The reality is that many European countries have not embraced multiculturalism, yet remain quite stubbornly unloved by their minorities. France's assimilationist politics has not made its North African-descended populations feel any more French, even though many of these families have been in France for several generations.

Rather, the difference is that European nations have never managed to escape an identity based on culture, ethnicity, language and religion. To be German was to be *Germanic* – white, German-speaking and Christian.

That, of course, was always an artificial national identity, but it was less so in a pre-globalised world of relative homogeneity. Today, however, we are witnessing the incompatibility of that approach with the globalised pluralism that is now irrepressible. Today, Germany is struggling desperately to decide in what way a Turkish migrant can ever be a German. Such a question sounds odd to Australian ears, and positively incomprehensible to American ones. That is because American identity is neither ethnic nor cultural: it is civil. America is simply too diverse a nation to have a common culture. Yet America manages to retain a coherent national identity in the face of this diversity because it gathers not around a comprehensive social culture, but a political idea: individual liberty, which is to say, liberalism. That, of course, includes the freedom to determine one's own cultural and moral values. The message to America's minorities, then, is not "assimilate," but "participate." Whatever one thinks of liberalism, this at least provides a conceptual framework that offers everyone a stake in the nation — no matter how shallow their historical and cultural connections to the country. It is a permeable national idea, not an exclusionary one. America remains a nation of wildly divergent value systems, from the most cosmopolitan to the most irascible and prejudiced. It is a nation of opposites, but it is loved by many people with almost nothing in common: white supremacists and African-Americans alike.

America's minorities feel American, yet jealously guard their hyphenated identities. They are, and remain, Italian-Americans, Latino-Americans, African-Americans, Jewish-Americans and Irish-Americans. The secret of a civil national identity is that it allows citizens the chance to sustain multiple identities simultaneously and in harmony. This contrasts with the neo-conservative ultimatum that requires each citizen to proclaim the primacy of their national identity to the exclusion of all else. What neo-conservatives do not understand, and what conservatives should, is that when presented with such an ultimatum, some (perhaps many) will simply choose to reject their national identity in a hostile fashion. That is hardly conducive to a sustainable national identity in our globalised, highly pluralist age.

Australia is not locked into Europe's ethno-cultural approach. Europe has little choice because this is simply how those societies have evolved. Australia, being a young, immigrant country, has a degree of choice in this matter – at least in the terms it uses to describe itself. A liberal conservative who recognises the impossibility of fabricating a new cultural homogeneity should surely see the wisdom in an American-style model, anchored in liberalism. It allows philosophical consistency, while providing a national narrative around which the nation can cohere. To be sure, this does not mean the importation of every American social structure. We can do without its levels of inequality and violence. We can do without its proclivity for neo-liberalism. But we may benefit from its lessons on national identity; and learn that for a national identity to find a place in the hearts of a diverse population – and remain coherent in an era of rapid migration and globalisation – it is best constructed on civic ideals and an ethos of participation, not cultural assimilation.

This does not mean the State should be value-free. Quite the opposite is true: the State should reflect important values in its conduct and its institutions. Consistent with the liberal conservative tradition, those values will be primarily institutional. But to the extent they are substantive, as with a value of gender equality, they should not be expressed coercively or didactically. The State will not fund or proactively support sexism, but it will not monitor its citizens for sexist attitudes, either.

For all his common ground with, and admiration for, John Howard, Tony Abbott does seem to have some grasp of this. When the neo-conservative cultural politics of the Howard era was at its most bellicose, Abbott took a more nuanced, typically liberal conservative position, writing in the Liberal Party journal, *The Party Room*:

> Nostalgia for when "everyone was pretty much the same" is a near universal characteristic – except that there almost certainly never

has been such a time, at least not in our country, nor in countries such as Britain and the US with a similar tradition of easygoing tolerance and social diversity ...

The dreadful spectacle of UK-born Muslims perpetrating terrorist atrocities against their fellow Britons has fuelled local calls for some kind of "Australian-ness" test, whether it be longer residence to qualify for citizenship, more prescriptive oaths of allegiance or greater English language fluency. Unfortunately, these inevitably reinforce the "them and us" mindset in which terrorism might ultimately thrive.

In the age of terror, it makes sense to ban incitement to violence or membership of organisations dedicated to violence, but it makes very little sense to alienate large numbers of people who are Australian citizens and who are adapting to Australian society in their own way and at their own pace. Disparaging the religious symbols of Muslim Australians is at odds with our own best traditions. Why should Muslims turn out to be resistant to the gravitational pull of the Australian way of life when no one else has?

Abbott speaks like a man who understands what it is to belong to a once-maligned religious minority. In his recent Australia Day speech, he cited the unfailingly controversial example of Sheikh Taj al-Din al-Hilali, and followed up immediately with a reference to the Catholic archbishop Daniel Mannix, whose statements during World War I saw calls for him to be deported. "There has hardly been a time when there were not some reservations about the loyalty of particular ethnic or religious groups," observed Abbott. "A generation or two on, all of them have eventually become as Australian as everyone else." This is a very different tone from Howard's, even if the elements of Abbott's speech dealing with asylum seekers showed Howard's cultural legacy would remain to some degree.

Abbott lists among his heroes Bob Santamaria, a legend of Australian conservatism who, possibly because of his Catholicism, had many social values in common with Abbott. But Santamaria was too consistent in his conservatism to embrace neo-liberalism. He was a fierce critic of capitalism, appalled at the materialism it implies, the inequalities it produces and its unprincipled violations of Catholic social teachings. In this respect, Abbott is closer to Howard: a staunch defender of capitalism and a believer in its political virtues. If Abbott is able to move beyond the knee-jerk opposition he presently seems to advocate, it will be intriguing to see how he manages these ideological sympathies. If he can, the contradictory but symbiotic relationship between neo-liberalism and neo-conservatism will persist for a while yet. That is especially true if Abbott's term is a success. If not, the future of Australian conservative politics may well be shaped by an entirely different worldview. Given the Liberal Party's tendency to be a creature of its successful leaders, its direction is unlikely to be known until it finds its next prime minister.

The sketch I have given here of a renewed liberal conservatism is broad and preliminary. It is certainly not intended to be definitive. Undoubtedly, as it is unpacked further, ambiguities and shortcomings will arise. What is certain is that it is time to conceive of a politics that leaves behind neo-liberal neo-conservatism in search of something less reactionary and more principled. No doubt this will be an immensely difficult task, particularly in Australia where traditional conservatism seems crushingly absent at present, but that does not make it any less imperative.

SOURCES

1   "Is Castro left-wing or right-wing? Explain your answer": Andrew Kenny, "The End of Left and Right," *The Spectator*, Vol. 297, No. 9209, 5 February 2005, 18–19.

2   "how much they hated each other": Kenny, "The End of Left and Right," 18.

4   "deserves thoughtful investigation": Kenny, "The End of Left and Right," 19.

8   "What brought Conservatism into existence": Lord Hugh Cecil, *Conservatism* (London: Home University Library, 1912), 39.

8   "cant and gibberish of hypocrisy": Edmund Burke, *Reflections on the Revolution in France* (London: Rivingtons, 1868), 120.

8   "sentiments of morality and religion": Burke, *Reflections on the Revolution in France*, 175.

8   "an inheritance from our forefathers": Burke, *Reflections on the Revolution in France*, 40.

9   "abstract principle": Burke, *Reflections on the Revolution in France*, 21.

9   "our rights and privileges": Burke, *Reflections on the Revolution in France*, 43–44.

10   "before his eyes": Burke, *Reflections on the Revolution in France*, 73.

10   "means of its conservation": Burke, *Reflections on the Revolution in France*, 29.

10   "religiously to preserve": Burke, *Reflections on the Revolution in France*, 29.

11   "duty of future Conservatives to defend": Quintin Hogg, *The Case for Conservatism* (Hammondsworth: Penguin Books, 1947), 14.

11   "must disintegrate in time": Paul Smith (ed), *Lord Salisbury on Politics* (Cambridge: Cambridge University Press, 1972), 106.

12   "between wisdom and folly": Cited in Phillip W. Buck (ed), *How Conservatives Think* (Hammondsworth: Penguin Books, 1975), 21.

12   "the captainless many": Cited in Phillip W. Buck (ed), *How Conservatives Think*, 20.

13   "steady supporters of liberty": William Edward Hartpole Lecky, *Democracy and Liberty*, Vol. 1 (London: Longmans, Green, and Co, 1896), 214, 215.

13   "as well as you can": Alexis de Tocqueville, *Democracy in America*, Vol. 1, trans. Henry Reeve, Esq. (Cambridge: Sever and Francis, 1864), 332.

13   "bound to come": Blanche Elizabeth Campbell Dugdale, *Arthur James Balfour, First Earl of Balfour, K.G., O.M., F.R.S., etc*, Vol. 1 (New York: G.P. Putnam's Sons, 1937), 52.

14   "to violate the laws": Edmund Burke, *Thoughts on the Cause of the Present Discontents* (London: J. Dodsley, 1784), 41.

14   "an attitude of mind": Baron Richard Kidston Law Coleraine, *For Conservatives Only* (London: Tom Stacey Ltd, 1970), 20.

15   "all subjects alike": Michael Oakeshott, "On Being Conservative," in *Rationalism in Politics* (London: Shenval Press Ltd, 1962), 168–196, 188.

15   "leading to error ...": Michael Oakeshott, "On Being Conservative," 195.

15   "Conservatism is of course": Lord Hugh Cecil, *Conservatism*, 246–249.

18   "permanent source of improvement": John Stuart Mill, *On Liberty* (London: Longmans, Green, and Co., 1867), 41.

18   "hindrance to human advancement": Mill, *On Liberty*, 41.

18   "at something better than customary": Mill, *On Liberty*, 41.

18   "experiments of living": Mill, *On Liberty*, 33.

18   "political or social reform": Lord Hugh Cecil, *Conservatism*, 48.

18   "moral and social reformers": Mill, *On Liberty*, 33.

19   "right of spiritual domination": Mill, *On Liberty*, 8.

19   "on an unwilling people": Mill, *On Liberty*, 41.

20   "Socialist panacea": Robert Menzies, *Afternoon Light* (London: Cassell, 1967), 286.

21   "experience of our political party": Excerpts from the speech published in *The Conservative*, February 2006, No. 2, 40.

22   "desire to improve and elevate it": Benjamin Disraeli, "Speech at the Banquet of the National Union of Conservative and Constitutional Associations, 24 June 1872," in Buck (ed.), *How Conservatives Think*, 70–71, 71.

22   "humanise their toil": Disraeli, 'Speech at the Banquet of the National Union of Conservative and Constitutional Associations, 24 June 1872', 71.

22   "raise the condition of the poor": Lord Hugh Cecil, *Conservatism*, 245.

23   "where they wished to do so": Liberal and National Parties, *Future Directions: It's a Time for Plain Thinking* (December 1988), 96.

24   "something that can be imposed": Cited in Judith Brett, *Quarterly Essay 19, Relaxed & Comfortable: The Liberal Party's Australia* (Melbourne: Black Inc., 2005), 32–33.

25   "individual exertion and development": Mill, *On Liberty*, 68.

25   "young and vast country": Robert Menzies, *The Measure of the Years* (Melbourne: Cassell Australia, 1970), 35.

25   "private entrepreneurs can build": Menzies, *The Measure of the Years*, 36.

25   "labour force": John Hirst, "The Distinctiveness of Australian Democracy," in *Sense and Nonsense in Australian History* (Melbourne: Black Inc., 2009), 292–312, 307.

27   "the formation of private power": Cited in Edward N. Megay, "Anti-Pluralist Liberalism: The German Neoliberals," in *Political Science Quarterly*, Vol. 85, No. 3 (New York: Academy of Political Science, September, 1970), 422–442, 430.

28   "replete with abuses of power": Megay, "Anti-Pluralist Liberalism," 431.

29   "conservatism which deserves to be called such": Friedrich A. Hayek, "Why I Am Not a Conservative," in Gregory L. Schneider (ed), *Conservatism in America Since 1930* (New York: New York University Press, 2003), 180–194, 181.

29   "in which we are moving": Hayek, "Why I Am Not a Conservative," 181.

31   "performed some action": Friedrich Hayek, *Law, Legislation and Liberty*, Vol. 2, *The Mirage of Social Justice* (London: Routledge, 1976), 33.

33   "are purely 'economic'": Friedrich Hayek, *The Mirage of Social Justice*, 112.

33   "arising out of pecuniary interests": Cited in Albion W. Small, "Some Structural Material for the Idea 'Democracy,'" in *The Journal of American Sociology*, Vol. 25, No. 3 (Chicago: The University of Chicago Press, November, 1919), 257–297, 269.

36   "make mankind One World": Hayek, *The Mirage of Social Justice*, 112.

37   "the same style of politics": Michael Oakeshott, "Rationalism in Politics," in *Rationalism in Politics* (London: Shenval Press Ltd, 1962), 1–36, 21.

39   "This is what we believe": John Ranelagh, *Thatcher's People: An insider's account of the politics, the power and the personalities* (London: Fontana Press, 1992), ix.

41   "on the ash-heap of history": Ronald Reagan, "Address to Members of the British Parliament, Palace of Westminster, June 8, 1982," in Ronald Reagan, *Speaking My Mind: Selected Speeches* (New York: Simon and Schuster, 1989). 107–120, 118.

44   "the American cities under Reagan": Paul Kelly, *The End of Certainty* (St Leonard's: Allen & Unwin, 1992), 269.

45   "to embrace market liberalism": "John Howard – neo-liberal and social conservative," *Hindsight*, ABC Radio National, 22 April 2007.

46   "our industrial-relations system": Cited in Paul Kelly, *The End of Certainty*, 259–260.

47   "the faith and fortitude of the next generation": Ronald Reagan, "Address to Members of the British Parliament, 8 June 1982," 120.

50   "favours from powerful customers": Iran Kastev, "The Greengrocer's Revenge," *Prospect*, No. 163, 23 September 2009.

51   "IMF guidelines without debate": Joseph Stiglitz, *Globalization and its Discontents* (London: Penguin, 2002), xiii–xiv.

52   "no longer understood by contemporary conservatives": John Gray, *Enlightenment's Wake: Politics and culture at the close of the modern age* (London: Routledge, 1995), 87.

53   "traditional institutions and professions": Gray, *Enlightenment's Wake*, 87.

55   "and of public morality": Emma Rush and Andrea La Nauze, *Corporate Paedophilia: Sexualisation of children in Australia* (Canberra: The Australia Institute, 2006), vii.

55   "moral panic": Editorial, *The Australian*, 12 October 2006.

59   "tragic for this country": Hansard, House of Representatives, 8 May 1984, 2020.

60   "people of this country": Hansard, House of Representatives, 8 May 1984, 2024.

61   "integration could not be achieved": Paul Kelly, *The End of Certainty*, 674.

65   "major say in how it is exercised": Irving Kristol, *Neo-conservatism: The Autobiography of an Idea* (New York: The Free Press, 1999), 208.

65   "upper levels of the government bureaucracy": Kristol, *Neo-conservatism*, 207.

67   "cultural suicide pact": Editorial, "The veiled conceit of multiculturalism," *The Australian*, 24 October 2006.

67   "squalor and vulgarity on the streets": Melanie Phillips, *Londonistan* (New York: Encounter Books, 2006), xx.

68   "accept minority status": Melanie Phillips, *Londonistan*, xxiii.

68   "as conquerors": Editorial, "Taxi rank offence," *The Australian*, 2 October 2006.

68   "overturn our values": "Bronwyn Bishop responds to the Aussie Mossie," *The National Interest*, ABC Radio National, 28 August 2005.

69   "clear off": "Teach Australian values of 'clear off,' says Nelson," PM, ABC Radio National, 24 August 2005.

69   "rest of the Australian community": Michelle Grattan, "Accept Australian values or get out," *The Age*, 25 August 2005.

69   "equality of men and women": "PM tells Muslims to learn English," *The Australian*, 1 September 2006.

70   "scientific, moral, or theological": Mill, *On Liberty*, 7.

70   "many kinds of political oppression": Mill, *On Liberty*, 3.

71   "justified in silencing mankind": Mill, *On Liberty*, 10.

72   "never something that can be imposed": Brett, *Relaxed & Comfortable*, 32–33.

72   "accept Australian values and beliefs": Grattan, "Accept Australian values or get out," 25 August 2005.

74   "no special rules apply": Janet Albrechtsen, "Multicultural madness needs such antidotes," *The Australian*, 18 October 2006.

74   "values they must accept": See for example Janet Albrechtsen, "Open market on democratic ideals," *The Australian*, 3 May 2006.

79   "also appropriate for the times": Annabel Crabb, *Quarterly Essay 34, Stop at Nothing: The Life and Adventures of Malcolm Turnbull* (Melbourne: Black Inc., 2009), 62.

82   "[migrants'] ability to contribute": Mischa Schubert, "Andrews calls for debate over Muslim 'enclaves,'" *The Age*, 30 October 2009.

82   "treated exactly the same way": "A classic Q&A," Q&A, ABC Television, 26 February 2009.

83   "as many Muslim women do": Joe Hockey, "In Defence of God," address to the Sydney Institute, 9 November 2009.

83   "one of our greatest strengths": "The Youth Show," Q&A, ABC Television, 6 August 2009.

90   "their new religion": "Malcolm and the Malcontents," *Four Corners*, ABC Television, 9 November 2009.

90   "control or to rig the market": "Climate wars – Lord Monckton visits Australia," *The 7.30 Report*, ABC Television, 3 February 2010.

91   "Hitler Youth": "Climate wars – Lord Monckton visits Australia," *The 7.30 Report*.

93 "emissions intensity": "Tony Abbott joins *The 7.30 Report*," *The 7.30 Report*, ABC Television, 2 February 2010.

93 "in exceptional circumstances": "Abbott Plan," available at resources.news.com.au /files/2010/02/02/1225825/989703-abbott-plan.pdf, 14.

96 "old economic orthodoxy": David Cameron, "We need popular capitalism," speech to Davos, 30 January 2009.

96 "legislation to stop it": Rosa Prince, "David Cameron: Family matters to children more than income," *The Daily Telegraph Online* (London), 11 January 2010.

99 "lacking in law and property rights": John Gray, *Beyond the New Right: Markets, government and the common environment* (London: Routledge, 1993), 132–133.

102 "rights of the individual": Geoffrey Brahm Levey, "The Antidote of Multiculturalism," *Griffith Review*, Issue 15, 2007, 197–208, 201.

102 "I have argued elsewhere": Waleed Aly, "Patriot Acts," *The Monthly*, June 2009.

105 "way of life when no one else has?": Cited in Tony Abbott, "No worries, mate – Muslims will naturally integrate," *The Australian*, 2 November 2005.

105 "as Australian as everyone else": Tony Abbott, "Address to the Australia Day Council (Victoria) Australia Day Dinner," 22 January 2010.

NOTICE

In *Quarterly Essay* 35, we published a letter that said that Mr George Newhouse had failed to register properly as Labor candidate for the seat of Wentworth. That has been taken to impute that Mr Newhouse had failed to properly nominate as a candidate at the last federal election. We accept that this was not the case and apologise to Mr Newhouse.

Katharine Murphy

Mungo MacCallum presents an intriguing notion. To understand Kevin Rudd's popularity we should delve into the myths and the values of an Australia past. Another perspective can be found by rooting the prime minister firmly in Australia present. This exercise begins in a location MacCallum would more than likely approve of, a pub in Rockdale on a warm January night in 2010.

Gathered at the pub is a group of sisters and their spouses, downing pub tucker and quaffing an overly emphatic sav blanc from New Zealand. The party had pulled up to their watering hole in a people mover manufactured in Korea. They made their way past families talking in multiple languages in order to find a quieter spot. They are saying goodbye to one of their number. She and the bloke are off to Europe for a couple of years.

This group of Aussie women has Irish ancestry. They have EU passports and the convenience of long visas. All of them around the table have placed a premium on getting out and about in the world as both rite of passage and professional necessity. All – particularly the latest evacuee, just thirty years old in her designer jeans and Havaianas – see themselves as inhabitants of the globe, not exclusively of a continent at the bottom-end of nowhere.

The conversation is free-wheeling. Some of it is love and some is combat, that being the nature of sisters who enjoy the sound of their own voices. There is an examination of the merits of iPhones versus Blackberrys. The evacuee is very disappointed with her favourite director, Spike Jonze. *Where the Wild Things Are* is a disaster. No, it's not, counters the eldest one, fortified by fermented grapes from the Marlborough region. You are just too young and too old to understand the underlying sensibility.

It's late when the subject of Kevin comes up. A tween in the party rolls her eyes at this familiar and unwelcome conversational cul-de-sac. She lives in a house with political journalists and he comes up quite a bit around the dinner table.

Wisely she seeks out dessert while the latest assessments are sought.

The evacuee and her bloke approve of Kevin. They are not ideological. They are not joiners or believers. Who is these days? They engage with politics to the extent they can with busy professional and social lives. They work for themselves and they see the world in terms of creative clusters. The prime minister is getting on with things. He did what he said he'd do. He seems to know what matters, global things, like climate change and security.

Whether they like him is irrelevant. This sentiment is far more distant: it is approval and respect. His modern sensibility validates theirs – the time-zone hopping, his all-nighters to hit the deadline, his general seriousness about success, the nerdy stuff on Twitter.

The young woman and her bloke are so enamoured they will give him possibly thirty whole seconds more thought before leaving the country of their birth for an unspecified period. Sure, they'll miss their old house by the river and their friends and their scrapping family ... but actually not that much because everything is connected. A sneeze at Lehman Brothers causes an earthquake in Iceland. There is always Google chat.

Like Kevin, these two are citizens of the world, but unlike Kevin they don't have to do community cabinets in Tamworth or school visits in Port Augusta or show up at the Boxing Day Test in order to cover up their guilty secret. They can be porous and blissfully unencumbered.

The idea of nation and Australianness? Well, that's interesting, in some abstract sense, but when did nation ever define anyone or break anyone's heart?

Which leads me back to the problem of Mungo MacCallum. The problem with Mungo is you can't read anything he writes without feeling the need to agree with it on the spot, and wish you'd written it yourself.

Reading Mungo is like resisting the pull of a great seducer. There is the elegant prose. Silly political pretensions are cut through. New ideas emerge and fresh perspectives are offered, given this man loves to play outsider. Even when he was inside, the perspective was always outside the box.

This time we have Rudd rendered in myths and Australian nationhood. Lulled by the undulating structure of his essay, I declare him right. I float on his argument. It's those tropes and narratives of the past, stupid. Voters like Kevin Rudd because he is resolving the great Australian paradox. We are larrikins, but we feel most comfortable being told what to do. Of course people like him because he appeals to Australian myths and values, unobtrusively, blurring the difference with John Howard's narrative. He's a drover despite his soft white hands and his predilection for German theologians and acronyms.

He is Kevin from Queensland, that most parochial of places, and he is here to help.

Except … I shake myself vigorously to impose a discipline. Is that the person you see? Is there a *Eureka!* moment in here?

No, there isn't, I'm afraid. Here I am, one of Mungo's cursed "commentariat," I expect. One of the lazy knockers of Canberra's parliamentary press gallery, "bewildered" by Kevin Rudd, unable to see the true picture.

But MacCallum's essay reads to me like a thesis in search of a subject. Even as the technique imposes coherence and soothes and challenges the reader, he seems to know he's pushing it in places. As thoughtful and compelling as it is as a piece of argument to ponder over the summer before a federal election, for me this picture doesn't settle Rudd's protean political personality.

"For all his nerdiness and prolixity, there is something very *Australian* about him," Mungo tells us. I'm not sure that declaration would pass the front-bar test – not in the Australia of leather-skinned men who brush flies from their faces and talk without moving their lips.

Which Australia are we talking about? Rudd is without question a creature of the Australia of Converse high-tops and iPods and double degrees in international relations, but I can't see him fashioning the 2020 Summit on the sidelines of the Eureka Stockade.

Reading Mungo's essay I have a strange and satisfying sense of the Kevin Rudd rendered in the pages of *Quarterly Essay* straining impatiently against the implied weight of historical comparison – this relentless creature, who can't settle for a moment in the present, having to endure like Gulliver in Lilliput, lying prone in restraints as others conduct their worthy anthropology.

Kevin Rudd is always chasing the future, that much we can say. His boredom with the here and now would offend people if he weren't so adept at masking it.

When he declared peace in the history wars in 2009, the declaration was a clarion call to move on, rather than a piece of nifty political or intellectual positioning. Saying sorry to indigenous Australians, as profound as that moment was, was hurry up and move on as well; move on to solving social and economic disadvantage. Move on. Always move on.

The thing that is fascinating about Rudd is how far he has eclipsed his origins, how far he has travelled from the suffocating provincialism of the Queensland of his childhood. He is still running from it into something bigger, with all his ambition to be in the next place, in the next conversation, on the next plane to the next time zone, in the next hospital or on the next street walk doing the retail politics.

MacCallum is right when he concludes the prime minister is an enlarger. With his compulsive restlessness he cannot be anything else.

It's been fun for Mungo to think of Rudd in an Australian tradition, droving his way through marginal seats, giving us back our "Lucky Country," winning over hearts and minds in the process. It's been constructive, too, that discipline. Get off the Rudd bus and look back to achieve a new perspective; look at him from another angle.

But I can't position him in that space. The vexatious bugger, he just won't stay there. The key to Rudd's success with the voters, I fear, is far more prosaic. Boring even. Kevin Rudd's popularity is notable, certainly, but not all that mysterious, given voters took a significant chance in 2007 by putting him in the Lodge. So far he has made good on their investment by being competent and methodical, and by fine-tuning the country to reflect the current mood.

He has used the global economic crisis to his advantage politically; and the government was assisted not only by the early warning of impending disaster but also by sound policy advice and by a budget bequeathed in good order, which allowed scope for a textbook Keynesian response.

The government's focus on keeping the probable rise in unemployment to a minimum was as much, in my view, about learning from the mistakes of the Keating government in the early 1990s as it was a genuflection to the importance of jobs and a living wage in the Australian social compact.

Most of all, Kevin Rudd has been assisted by a bruised and riven Opposition, which has given a government-in-training space to learn its craft without significant obstruction, except of course in the Senate, and that drama will play out to its conclusion in 2010.

See? Prosaic. I did warn you.

Perhaps, given this mundane reality, the only answer is to embrace MacCallum's trope of Rudd as a descendant of characters in the Australian legend, from the bushman and the drover to the shearers of Barcaldine. It is far more interesting.

But none of us should lose heart. Kevin Rudd is still in many respects a blank canvas. This history is still being written. He plays politics defensively enough for voters to have ample room to project their own aspirations onto him. Unlike John Howard, Kevin Rudd does wait for the times to suit him; at his sharpest, he has the dexterity to adjust to suit the times.

He will go on evolving despite our attempts to explain him and render him explicable, this slave to the future, this international man of mystery, this Twitter nerd, this man in a blazing bloody hurry.

Katharine Murphy

Greg Melleuish

Mungo MacCallum takes a meandering walk through a highly impressionistic story of Australia to answer what for many of us, including, I think, Mungo, is the great puzzle of contemporary Australian politics: what exactly is it that makes Kevin Rudd so popular? By the end of his excursion he manages to convince himself that he has discovered "Kevin's secret." This is that Kevin has given Australians "back their Lucky Country … he took them back to the bedrock of their legends, their values and their dreams." They believe that he has "integrity" and they can "trust" what he is doing.

Now Mungo, after working himself up into a bit of a lather, after quoting an amount of bush poetry in an effort to demonstrate that Kevin is an heir to THE Australian tradition, may believe this to be the case. But I, for one, remain unconvinced. The puzzle of Rudd remains. The puzzle remains, I think, because the method is all wrong. I do not think that there is much to be gained by linking Rudd to a highly romantic and mythological account of the Australian story. Rudd is not like a figure out of Banjo Paterson; he is not Dad Rudd MP (and I wonder why no one has shown this movie in the last couple of years). Rudd is a highly skilled professional politician with a lot of experience as an administrator. He is a man who earned the nickname "Dr Death" when he worked for Wayne Goss.

If anything, the key to understanding Rudd lies in the direction that Australian politics has taken over the past twenty years in relation to the *longue durée* of Australian historical development. Rudd is not the first politician of his type to emerge in Australia: both Bob Carr and John Howard may be considered to be antecedents. Neither of them conformed to the "Australian legend" and yet they were both supremely successful politicians. The point is that the days of Henry Bolte and Robert Askin, larger-than-life figures who perhaps did owe something to the Australian legend, are gone, never to return, even in Queensland.

The central issue is the task of the leader in a democratic society at a time when the role of government has become increasingly complex, and the demands placed on government ever greater. It is, of course, one of the great myths surrounding "neo-liberalism" that governments have done less and less over the past twenty-five years. Even as they attempted to privatise and reduce their activity, they found themselves legislating more, regulating more and doing more. The real issue is the extent to which they can actually do all that is desired of them, as opposed merely to appearing to have everything under control.

Australia, we are constantly reminded, is one of the oldest democracies in the world. Its political leaders have to operate as the leaders of a democracy. They must act in accord with the general wishes of the majority or face the consequences. The settlement that came into being after Federation expressed the desires of Australian democracy. Its primary desire was to protect the interests of that small number of Australians of largely British descent then living here. Hence it had a desire to exclude those who were different, and to create mechanisms that would ensure a "modest comfort" for most people living in Australia.

Mungo is correct: it was concerned with "jobs, jobs, jobs." Its policies of racial exclusion, tariff protection and arbitration were extremely popular. But they can hardly be described as idealistic. They were selfish policies that worked by passing the costs of Australian egalitarianism onto other groups. These included producers in other countries and Australian farmers. Peter Spencer is not the first rural victim of egalitarian urban Australia.

More importantly, as W.K. Hancock demonstrated in his classic *Australia*, these policies were not particularly effective and were only able to be sustained because Australia was rich in resources in relation to its small population. They became unsustainable as the Australian population increased over the next fifty years. The crunch came in the 1980s when a Labor government instituted "neo-liberal" policies, not out of ideology but necessity. These liberal policies were not popular with the wider electorate; they were something to be endured rather than loved (as White Australia had once been).

The message from the government in the years since 1983 has been that we should all do more for ourselves. The desire of the democratic electorate has been that government should interest itself even more in voters' welfare; it should protect them from the many evils that are out there in the world. However, the capacity of the government to do this is limited, especially as it finds itself committed to cutting taxes in the name of encouraging individuals to take responsibility for their lives.

The consequence is, I believe, a new type of democratic politician who must appear to be doing a lot, even as they find themselves limited in what they can do. They employ media consultants and spin doctors to ensure that they have the appropriate public image and are popular. They engage in activity, as Sir Humphrey pointed out many years ago, as a substitute for achievement.

Rudd has followed in the footsteps of Howard in that he no longer sees himself as just a political leader but rather as some sort of moral authority benevolently issuing advice, like a local equivalent of Dr Phil, on all sorts of matters, including the behaviour of Kyle and Jackie O. This type of democratic politician can, if he is effective, soothe the worries and concerns of the electorate and make voters feel that they are being protected. Kevin, like John before him, becomes a benevolent uncle with whom one can feel safe.

The triumph of appearance over reality does have its costs. The problems to which Hawke and Keating responded in 1983 have not gone away; and there can be no going back, thankfully, to the policies of an earlier era. It is not in the best interests of the electorate to be serenaded into complacency. This is best demonstrated by the example of Bob Carr, who may be regarded as Kevin's role model. Bob was very good at being re-elected in New South Wales, and he had all the gifts required of a democratic politician of the early twenty-first century. He appeared to be doing things. But one has only to look at New South Wales in 2010 to realise the ultimate consequence of that sort of politics. And there appears to be very little light at the end of the tunnel.

Of course, we may yet receive another dose of the "Lucky Country" as we ride the Chinese tiger. Just as in the early twentieth century Australia could afford its poor policies because it was rich, so early twenty-first century Australia may yet be able to use its Chinese connections to support its illusions and its do-nothing political leaders. The day of reckoning may be able to be put off for some time, but there will eventually be another 1983. Then Australians will need political leaders who can actually do something beyond soothing us with honeyed words.

Greg Melleuish

Tim Soutphommasane

Reading Mungo MacCallum's *Quarterly Essay* of last year for a second time in January, I wondered whether he might have changed anything had he written it after Tony Abbott claimed the Liberal Party leadership. The motif of MacCallum's essay is, of course, the Australian Story. His thesis: that a great deal of Rudd's political success has been bound up in his judicious appropriation of Australian cultural myths. How, then, might MacCallum respond to the suggestion that the emergence of Abbott as Liberal leader neutralises such an advantage of Rudd's?

In terms of cultural authenticity, Abbott undoubtedly poses a more formidable challenge to Rudd than Brendan Nelson or Malcolm Turnbull ever could. Commentators, particularly those who lean to the Right, have certainly been excited by Abbott's leadership. After all, not since the days of Robert James Lee Hawke has a national politician paraded so proudly before cameras in budgie-smugglers. Authenticity is that rarest of political assets these days, although, of course, it can never on its own guarantee electoral success.

MacCallum's rich and refreshing essay makes a thought-provoking claim in suggesting that Rudd has all this time been quietly cultivating an Australian authenticity. Our prime minister is not a technocrat concerned only with power, process and efficiency, as commentators frequently suggest, but a leader who acts squarely within the national tradition.

MacCallum has done us a service in placing the Rudd prime ministership in some historical context. A long view of Australian politics is sadly one that our commentators do not offer us in the right doses. Too often, for instance, political slogans get mistaken for comprehensive narratives. When during the 2007 federal election campaign Rudd Labor adopted the phrase "new leadership," many quickly latched on to it as the narrative of Rudd's remarkable path to office. Excited by the prospect of the Howard years drawing to a close, many in our republic of letters believed a Rudd government would usher in a period of reinventing Australia.

Yet it was never entirely clear that "new leadership" would mean a "new Australia." The vision behind Rudd's case for office extended only to calculated signals of a reformist agenda rather than an exhaustive political program. Talk about a Rudd narrative was hopelessly premature, and the long honeymoon our new prime minister enjoyed well into 2008, if not also 2009, meant there was hardly a rush to articulate one.

Rudd has since found his narrative, however, with the global financial crisis. As Harold Macmillan would have said, "events" were the key. Ideologically, Rudd has emerged as a critic of free-market, neo-liberal capitalism, and an avowed Keynesian social democrat.

MacCallum's contribution is to propose that this story has a cultural under-pinning. It is "unfair," MacCallum argues, to judge that Rudd has failed to offer a coherent political narrative to replace John Howard's version of Australia. Rudd has "in fact embraced a great deal of the Australian tradition, in terms of both its myths and its values." On my count, MacCallum surveys at least six particular aspects of the Australian tradition that Rudd has tapped: an optimistic belief that we are the "Lucky Country"; a utilitarian preoccupation with jobs in our economic debates; a deep sense of egalitarianism; an equally deep yearning for stability; a cultural larrikinism; and a national self-understanding built on sport, mateship and the bush.

There is a danger in all this that we may overplay the extent to which Rudd has made himself and the Australian tradition one. At one point, for example, MacCallum suggests that Rudd's promise to end the "blame game" between the Commonwealth and the states in health care is motivated by a sense of a fair go and egalitarianism; a more plausible account would perhaps recognise that it is the goal of administrative efficiency and a belief in a strong central government that are the real sources of Rudd's pledge. But there are many other points at which MacCallum is surely right in his analysis. Nowhere is this more so than in his observations on WorkChoices, an area where Rudd was indeed able to make political gain by making himself "the champion who would restore justice and decency." Recall Rudd's declaration that he would not allow the fair go to be thrown "out the back door."

Yet Rudd is not, as far as anyone can tell, a cultural nationalist in the same way as, say, his Labor predecessor Paul Keating. With Keating there was an unvarnished radical nationalism, a direct lineage with Henry Lawson and Jack Lang. Rudd's confessed ideological influences are more pluralistic, ranging from Keir Hardie and Andrew Fisher to Dietrich Bonhoeffer to John Maynard Keynes. Moreover, the depths of such ideological attachments are not entirely clear, in part because Rudd remains, even though he is prime minister, a figure who has spent relatively little time in public office.

What is becoming increasingly clear, though, is that Rudd would like to position his government as a reformist, nation-building one. The language of nation-building dominated his government's response to the global financial crisis. Rudd has enthusiastically claimed a continuity with Hawke and Keating while brazenly thrashing the reform credentials of Howard and Costello. In a series of speeches in January this year, Rudd indicated his government would pursue a productivity agenda and declared this would be a "building decade" as part of a vision of a bigger Australia whose population will nudge 36 million by 2050.

Any judgment of the Rudd government's performance should naturally be made against the standard of nation-building reform. Here, Rudd faces some challenges. When used by Rudd and his ministers, nation-building has frequently been reduced to a synonym for physical infrastructure. A more discerning understanding of nation-building understands that it has both a "hard" and "soft" dimension – the latter referring to efforts to build a community of citizens. Thus understood, questions such as indigenous reconciliation, the republic and immigrant integration are also fundamentally nation-building concerns.

Another way of putting the matter is to say that the Rudd government stands at a curious juncture in Australian political history. The last three decades have been dominated by successive efforts to dismantle the Deakinite "Australian settlement" – an institutional and ideological system that offered a coherent vision of citizenship and community for much of the twentieth century. Yet no equivalent architecture has replaced it.

The Rudd government has an opportunity to reshape Australian political culture along social-democratic lines. But any ideological development beyond the Australian settlement may well be too traumatic. What MacCallum identifies as the Australian tradition might simply reflect the cultural residue of the settlement. If MacCallum is right about Rudd's authenticity, then Rudd may be more inclined to be culturally reassuring rather than radical.

In any case, any brand of social democracy pursued by Rudd is likely to disappoint some of the more quixotic within the Australian Left, as it will draw as much upon progressive liberalism as it will upon democratic socialism. Then again, social democracy has always been a hybrid political ideology grounded in practice rather than in doctrinal political philosophy. The heritage of modern social democracy can be traced both to socialism and liberalism.

This essay reminds us we should not easily dismiss Rudd as a nation-building prime minister. "Rudd would dearly love," MacCallum argues, "to recapture the heady optimism of those days [the Whitlam years], and one of the ways he is trying to use and modify the Australian tradition is to restore a sense of idealism; to persuade the so-called aspirational voters that there is more to aspire to than just moving up to a bigger McMansion."

Whether he can succeed in doing so is perhaps the big question, and it boils down to leadership.

The political scientist and historian James MacGregor Burns once distinguished between leaders who are transforming and those who are transactional. Transforming leaders were ones who elevated their followers to a different plane. They engaged with their followers' moral values. Transactional leaders, on the other hand, were ones who focused on engaging with followers' interests, and bargaining their way to results.

In their very different ways, both Paul Keating and John Howard exercised transforming leadership at particular moments during their respective times in office. For now, Rudd's transactional leadership cannot be faulted. Whether he can also be judged to be a transforming leader depends on whether he can fashion from the global financial crisis a compelling narrative for reform. This will need to draw upon not only the Australian tradition, but also the social-democratic tradition of which he has said he is part.

Tim Soutphommasane

Dennis Glover

Few commentators who remember the Whitlam and Keating years have much positive to say about anything Labor has done since. In fact, few former Labor leaders, cabinet ministers, advisers or even members have much positive to say either. When Labor's not betraying what it stands for, it's boring everyone witless. It's all just so unexciting, in the same way that victorious battles always seem dull compared to the charge of the Light Brigade. It would be all too easy to conclude that the whole point of the ALP is to produce tragic heroic narratives to inspire future generations of potential martyrs. So when *Quarterly Essay* 36 arrived, I thought "Here we go again," not for partisan reasons (although I'm a Labor member, former adviser and sometimes speechwriter), but because such critiques tend to miss the point of politics (which is to win power and change things) and give a misleading picture of the true nature of the Rudd government. Mungo MacCallum's essay, however, pleasantly surprised me. On one level, he's as bewildered as everyone else about what the government really stands for, but on another level he's grasped something important: in an essential way Rudd is a progressive. He may be neither a revolutionary nor a rabble-rousing orator, and has the ability to drive his own followers crazy with frustration. He may be cautious and sometimes conservative, but Kevin Rudd is definitely not a reactionary of the John Howard sort.

So what makes Kevin Rudd a progressive (or at least the sort of conservative modern progressive MacCallum believes he is)? MacCallum gets it pretty much right, but there's another dimension that is seldom discussed but which I believe should be: Rudd as a successful model of a modern social democrat.

To understand this you need to think about the ideological conflicts of the last few decades. One of the greatest sources of frustration to many Labor advisers during the Beazley, Crean and Latham years was the party's failure to see the value of devising a coherent alternative view of the world ("ideology" for want of a less alienating term) to that pushed so forcefully by the Howard government. Latham tried, sometimes, but only at the level of guerrilla warfare and without much strategy (and in many areas, such as social policy and economics, he was often closer to Howard than to his own party – as his current bi-weekly column in the *Australian Financial Review* demonstrates so comprehensively).

Discussing ideology may at first blush seem ridiculously academic, but it makes good practical political sense. It's true that ideology can bring out the worst in people and lead the unwise into the wilderness of perpetual opposition (like British Labour in the 1980s and perhaps the Abbott-led Coalition in the 2010s), but without an ideology to provide coherence to your story it's difficult to project the sorts of things voters value even more than policies, such as purposefulness, confidence and strength of character. Voters don't want their leaders to be ideological extremists, but they do want them to stand for something and provide a sense of direction for the nation. No one is going to vote for a flip-flopper who stands for what the pollsters just told him. Voters may have liked Kim Beazley's humanity, respected Simon Crean's gutsiness and occasionally admired Mark Latham's volcanic potential, but did they have any real idea of where any of these wanted to take the country? Paul Keating knew where he wanted to take the country (and obviously still does); it's just that, as Paul Kelly's latest book *The March of Patriots* argues well, it was not where the Australian people actually wanted to go.

The same cannot be said of the Howard government. John Howard might have been pragmatic, might have constantly bribed swinging voters, and might have ended up increasing the size of government to the fury of the Institute of Public Affairs and the Centre for Independent Studies, but he used ideology extremely effectively to project a sense of purpose and motivate his followers. ("You may not like him, but at least you know what he stands for." "You may not like the GST, but you know it's good for the country." "He may have lied about *Tampa*, but he turned the boats back.") At the risk of over-simplifying, we could reduce the Howard ideology to a few overarching propositions: the free market is unambiguously good; big government is unambiguously bad; equality is the enemy of prosperity; so is the environment; the elites are the enemy; and Australia is for "us." As I said, what actually occurred was often different from this, but we caught his drift for long enough, especially when it really counted, such as in 1996 and 2001 when circumstances required unsubtlety. Much of this can be put down to Howard's Menzian liberal-conservatism – as Judith Brett has argued here and elsewhere – but there's also little doubt that Howard's strategies owed a lot to the election-winning template created by the international right-wing movement, especially the US Republican Party's strategists Lee Atwater and Karl Rove. You could rename it "the Bush ideology" and be pretty much accurate.

After the defeat of Latham, a number of people on the fringes of the Labor movement had had enough of the party's failure to think deeply about just what it stood for in the twenty-first century, and a movement of sorts began to develop. New think-tanks were formed – some modernising, some pushing the same old Whitlam–Keating-era messages – with the idea of influencing the next Labor government. (This wasn't actually expected until the end of 2010, as few believed Labor could realistically win in 2007.) The goal was to help develop a coherent alternative ideology for the party: one that fused Labor's traditional egalitarian values with a modernising program that was electorally popular. The template if not the actual policy detail was similar to the projects that launched Bill Clinton and Tony Blair in the previous decade. "Another doomed project," the cynics thought, but from the beginning one person showed very keen interest: Kevin Michael Rudd. He attended fundraising activities, sought out ideas on policy and strategy from the best centre-left thinkers in the country to inform his speeches and essays, provided moral encouragement, and generally proved he was listening. It was the sort of attention Australian progressives hadn't received from federal Labor for many years. From these early days it became obvious to many of us engaged in these activities, even those like me who were well disposed towards Kim Beazley, that the future belonged to Rudd.

It's not difficult to see how this was smart politics, especially in the face of a government whose conservative beliefs were starting to seem old-fashioned, intolerant and, in the case of climate change, just plain ridiculous. But it was also good politics within the Labor caucus, which was seriously depressed about its prospects under a leader who had lost two previous elections (even though he had Labor consistently ahead in the polls). Here in Kevin Rudd was a contender who took ideas seriously, could think strategically, was tactically savvy, had abundant energy and wasn't burdened with blame for the failures of the past. He was potentially the ALP's Tony Blair in the younger, more innocent days when Blair could still be regarded as a radical and an election-winner. He believed in something not only recognisably "Labor" but futuristic and electorally plausible. And these facts had a powerful appeal to the Labor caucus. They may not have totally accounted for Rudd's defeat of Kim Beazley, but they were an essential element in it. Ultimately Rudd could project purpose and hope – because he could explain in a few sentences what he believed, where he wanted the country to go and how he proposed to get it there. This quest – to devise a centre-left populism capable of defeating the populism of the Right (although Rudd always rejected the term "populist") – was in fact an international political holy grail, and Rudd was the first to find it, which accounts for his brief rock-star persona abroad.

To those who knew him in opposition, Rudd's interest in ideas as prime minister wasn't at all surprising. Which other political figure would pop his head around your office door and attempt to converse with you in Latin? What did surprise was the extent of his willingness to take on the old neo-liberal and neo-conservative paradigm with a new, modernising, social-democratic alternative. Let's not overstate this. Many of the ideas that were subsequently developed into Labor's platform would have been apparent to Rudd himself for a long time, many owed as much to pragmatism and polling as to belief, and many were adopted and sold only partially and cautiously; but Rudd's dramatic essays in the *Monthly* demonstrated that he was willing to take on the Right by attacking their philosophical, economic and political assumptions and by countering with an equally coherent, alternative set of assumptions. We take this type of philosophical adventurousness for granted now that it's no longer novel, and are usually cynical about its value, but it's easy to forget how stunning it appeared at the time and how many ordinary people were nodding their heads and saying "Yeah." Just as importantly, Rudd's essays demonstrated that he was willing to forge an alliance of sorts with progressive opinion-formers who had just about given up on ever being listened to again by the Labor Party and who had totally given up on Kim Beazley after *Tampa* (even if Beazley's stance was in fact more oppositional and gutsier than was generally understood).

So what were Rudd's social-democratic assumptions? Broadly we could put Rudd's message as this (and some of these points are well picked up by Mac-Callum): the free market is good but not the totally out-of-control and immoral version pushed by Wall Street; all government can work better; equality and prosperity go hand in hand; so do environmental sustainability and prosperity; in the era of human capital, ignorance not elitism is the enemy; in the era of globalisation and the rise of Asia, Australia must be for "everyone." This seems to me a pretty good summation of what practical social democracy means today. If, as MacCallum points out, Rudd's persona is "more chartered accountant than great war leader," that's because his social-democratic philosophy is (often excessively) tethered to the "everything can be measured and reorganised" mantras of the modern management-consulting industry. The philosophy may be old-fashioned, but the means are contemporary. (Rudd in fact isn't a typical bureaucrat, as he is often accused of being; he finds bureaucracy disappointing and frustrating, which is why he so often seeks out alternative advice from the private sector, and why he appoints the most edgy and modernising public servants and university leaders to positions of high authority.) Rudd may sound like the chairman of McKinsey or Boston or Bain, but (and I can scarcely believe I'm writing this) some of the best reform ideas in the fields of education and health are now coming from the major consulting houses. Perhaps the complexity of the modern world, and the resulting difficulty in overcoming inertia without hard, grinding institutional change, means that Rudd's "boring through hard timber" approach is as good as we can hope for. (Whether it really works or proves to be just another passing policy fad, only time will tell.)

Mungo MacCallum's essay is neither this explicit nor this comprehensive in its assessment of what, for want of a better term, we could call the "Rudd ideology," but he wisely eschews the typical "Rudd the closet Tory," "Rudd the mindless Queensland bureaucrat," "Rudd the gutless do-nothing" lines of argument that have become instant clichés (even if by the end I'm guessing he's a little disappointed, as so many are). For instance, MacCallum recognises the good sense and egalitarian impulse behind Rudd's national reform agenda to improve the performance, efficiency and fairness of our hospitals, schools and other social programs. He sees a progressive Labor radicalism and reforming ambition in Rudd's support for the G-20 process — which is, finally, giving an economic say to national governments representing the vast majority of the world's citizens. And MacCallum spends much time assessing Rudd's cultural beliefs, recognising the political acumen in identifying with the nation's myths and symbols (something too many press-gallery reporters regard as a giant bore — or, as he puts it, as "elitist wankery"). To MacCallum, Rudd's persona as the helpful Queenslander combined with his bending of our national myths slightly to the Left is smart politics. It's not only an end in itself but also a clever means of keeping the voters interested during the dead time as the government's big-picture reform agenda (ever so) gradually gathers momentum and produces concrete achievements (probably some time during its second term).

To MacCallum, Rudd is a politically smart mix of nationalist and internationalist, a ground-breaking pioneer, a security-conscious conservative, a social radical and dreamer about generalised affluence in a future working-man's paradise. His nerdiness gives him the capacity to talk about this vision in a way that ordinary people can relate to. Particularly interesting is MacCallum's mention of the speech Rudd made at the launch of Tom Keneally's first volume of *Australians* in August 2009. To me this is a most revealing speech, because in it Rudd unveils an electorally plausible progressive take on our nation. To mention Paul Kelly's book again, Kelly shows how Keating and Howard both tried to appeal to the electorate with competing visions of Australia's past: Keating by rejecting the past and its myths, even Gallipoli; Howard by embracing it all, even the tragic fate of the Stolen Generations, as a positive. As Kelly points out, the first may have been therapeutic but it was also electoral suicide, and Labor paid a high price; the second was simply at odds with the twenty-first century. Rudd, however, has insisted that we recognise the good and the bad in Australia's past as a starting point for building a more progressive future. Sensibly, he's prepared to embrace but reinterpret those parts of the past that Labor has traditionally rejected. Take Gallipoli: you won't hear Rudd denouncing it as a blood sacrifice for imperialism or a symbol of the incompetence of the British ruling class, but it is possible to imagine him projecting the mateship displayed by the diggers as a symbol of Australia's egalitarian origins and a lesson for the future.

The hope for progressives is that MacCallum is correct, and that while Rudd's reforming agenda is taking a long, long time to show results, the people will stay with him long enough and the wait will be worth it. Certainly there's a strong social-democratic philosophy at the base of what Rudd is doing, alongside a good understanding of the down-to-earth values of the electorate. Sometimes the slow build-up and overwhelming assault is preferable to the suicidal charge into the valley of death which the old Labor Party was so good at.

Dennis Glover

David McKnight

In *Australian Story* Mungo MacCallum sets out to explain the continuing popularity of Kevin Rudd and his government. He argues that "it has to be more complicated than successful spin." His answer is that Kevin Rudd has been able to tap into the myths and values of an Australian ethos. He argues that Rudd "embodies more of the Australian tradition than the commentators are prepared to acknowledge."

To explain the tradition, MacCallum takes us on a journey through the history of Australia, beginning with the strikes of the 1890s, which spawned both the utopian colony in Paraguay and the Australian Labor Party. While acknowledging the massacres of indigenous people, it is largely a story of hope and progress in a new land, a story of Menzies and mateship, liberally spiced with bush poetry. In spite of the sentiment, MacCallum concludes that the Australian tradition involves both the larrikin outlaw and the dutiful citizen, both the expression of egalitarianism and of self-interest. Rudd has managed to divine the meaning of this dichotomy, to articulate a rhetoric around it and, somehow, this explains his popularity.

I'm not convinced that this is the real narrative of the Rudd government. A far better case can be made out that it was John Howard, not Kevin Rudd, who managed to use the Australian ethos to capture popular support. True, MacCallum argues that Rudd has done this more unobtrusively than Howard, and that Rudd has embellished, not rejected, Howard's narrative. But do you really need to invoke the Australian legend to understand Rudd and Labor's continuing success?

Howard actually believed in his version of the Australian legend of noble battlers and proud pioneers. The question raised by MacCallum's *Australian Story* is: What does Kevin Rudd actually believe in? MacCallum says that Rudd is "a pretty straightforward social democrat, accepting the broad tenets of capitalism provided it can be regulated in ways necessary to make it a tool of a civilised and compassionate society." At another point he says Rudd is "steeped in the Labor tradition." If this is so, then Rudd is taking the Labor tradition in an unusual direction.

Rudd's distinctiveness begins with the fact that ideas are more important to him than they are to most politicians. While his deepest engagement with ideas is around international relations, his most public claim has been his criticism of free-market fundamentalism. He sees himself as part of the tradition of social democracy but has staked out an ambitious claim to take it into new terrain.

Certainly something is needed, because this hundred-year-old tradition of political reform based on the working class has lost its way in the last twenty years. Its most fundamental values were the primacy of a common good and a scepticism about the social role of private enterprise. Translated into economic policy, this meant support for forms of public ownership, strong public institutions (in health and education) and a commitment to firm regulation of business. Supplemented by Keynesianism, social democrats ran deficit budgets to support these goals. But this legacy has been largely junked in Australia and elsewhere.

Rudd's own attempt to carve out new territory for social democracy was hinted at in several speeches while in opposition. He made a particularly revealing speech just before becoming Opposition leader in late 2006. Titled "What's Wrong with the Right," the speech was given to a free-market think-tank in Sydney, the Centre for Independent Studies. In this speech, long before the global financial crisis, Rudd presciently remarked that one of the tasks of social democrats was preventing "market capitalism from tearing itself apart through the destructive social and political forces it is capable of unleashing from time to time."

While attacking free-market fundamentalism and its prophet, the philosopher and economist Friedrich Hayek, the speech aimed to distance Hayek from Adam Smith, the thinker most commonly regarded as the source of liberal economics. The reason for this distinction was to allow Rudd to claim that Adam Smith was a major source of ideas for social democracy. It is a controversial claim. Social-democratic thinking, while diverse, originally grew from the European labour movement, influenced far more by Marx and other socialists. After 1917, European social democracy vigorously opposed revolutionary Marxism and opted for a mixed economy, but still not for Adam Smith.

Rudd pointed out that by Adam Smith's definition, education, health and the environment are public goods which the market usually can't provide. Social democrats could thus make common cause with him. The *delivery* of public goods was different, he said. "A cocktail of private and public delivery modes may be appropriate, depending on the relative cost-effectiveness in the physical delivery of the public goods in question."

Perhaps Rudd's public incorporation of Adam Smith in his own intellectual roots was done with the 2007 election in mind, but I doubt it. His policy direction in government suggests that it was more sincere than this. This can be seen in the particular policy device that is becoming a hallmark of the Rudd–Gillard government, which is the creation of what are called "quasi-markets." These are government-sponsored markets for government-supported services (education, health, social care) in which consumer-citizens choose from a range of providers (public or private). In this model, the theory is that consumer choice will induce higher standards in the service delivered by the providers.

The most far-reaching of these extensions to market mechanisms is Medicare Select, an option raised by Labor's review of health insurance and which would replace Medicare as we know it. It involves inviting private insurers into basic health provision and creating a competitive market between them. On this model, it is claimed, consumer choice of insurance will drive improved quality. Though sidelined for the moment, Medicare Select refuses to go away.

In Labor's plan for schools, competition between schools and parent choice will drive improvement based on league tables of school results. In post-secondary education, Labor encourages a form of voucher system, whose best-known advocate was the neo-liberal economist Milton Friedman. In vocational training, private colleges are increasingly encouraged to compete with TAFE. In universities, Labor has endorsed a student voucher mechanism for the future funding of this sector. In different but related ways, quasi-markets are being reinforced in aged care and child care. In most of these areas, private provision will grow, and public and charitable provision will retreat. It's all a massive Smithian gamble that the invisible hand and the private sector can be regulated so that they deliver quality services and equitable results in the Labor tradition. It runs counter to the social-democratic tradition of quarantining areas of society from the profit motive. It is a very long way from the kind of Labor tradition to which Mungo MacCallum refers.

Education is also the focus for the other set of ideas contributing to the Rudd government's distinctive version of social democracy. Human capital theory is the name of a body of economic thought which became popular after World War II. It identifies workers' skills and capacities as a basic source of a society's wealth and economic progress. Education, training and literacy are therefore a central concern for the theorists of human capital.

Rudd's enthusiasm for this was clear in Labor's pre-election policy for an "education revolution." The policy document's subtitle refers to "the critical link between long-term prosperity, productivity growth and human capital investment." The policy argues that Australia needs to turn its productivity performance around and enhance its workforce participation. In Rudd's 2006 speech, mentioned above, he justifies Labor's education revolution in the recognisable jargon of human capital theory: "If education and training become the engine room for equity in the social democratic project, this investment in human capital will enhance market performance by enhancing total factor productivity."

The influence of human capital theory can also be seen in two other areas of Labor's policy. Early childhood education is part of what is now referred to in Canberra as the government's "human capital agenda." Labor's education policy notes that in "areas like early childhood, Australia's education outcomes are falling well behind other nations ... investment in early childhood learning offers the greatest dividends." Most of us by now are so inured to this kind of language that we see nothing wrong with demanding "dividends" from early childhood. The other policy area is parental and maternity leave. The Productivity Commission noted that one of the three broad grounds for a paid parental-leave scheme was the "encouragement of women of reproductive ages to maintain their lifetime attachment to the workforce." During the public debate on this issue, supporters of maternity leave framed their rhetoric around the buzzwords of human capital theory. The Sex Discrimination Commissioner, Elizabeth Broderick, worried that the lack of maternity leave may cause "a serious leakage of human capital in the form of women leaving the workplace."

There is obviously nothing wrong with a desire to enrich the skills and education of the Australian workforce. With its focus on the worker and his or her skills, human capital theory has a special appeal for a party whose roots have workers and the workplace at its heart. It also makes sense, as ALP policy argued, that Australia should not simply be "China's quarry and Japan's beach" – we obviously do need an innovative, knowledge-based economy that can compete and win global markets.

But the problem is that when you reconstruct a social-democratic vision around Adam Smith and human capital theory, you invite the values of the market and self-interest into areas once quarantined from them. There is also something absent. Theories about the economy need to be underpinned by an ethical vision. And ultimately, Rudd's popularity will depend on voters' instincts about his ethical vision, about social justice and about fairness – the values underlying what's best in the Australian tradition that Mungo MacCallum examines – rather than technical economic theories.

David McKnight

Nick Bryant

Mark Twain once said of the music of Richard Wagner that it was much better than it sounds. The same is perhaps true of the politics of Kevin Rudd, with its voice-track of acronyms, faux larrikinisms and lifeless set-piece speeches. To the international eye, he comes across as thorough, well briefed and highly intelligent, but with a demeanour normally associated with Nordic prime ministers or Belgian finance chiefs. In their kingdoms of the mind, outsiders prefer Antipodean leaders to be rougher around the edges, with outsized personalities, prodigious drinking capabilities and a penchant for giving the entire country a day off at times of national celebration. Put another way, they expect the prime minister not only to govern but to personify Australia, or, at least, their misconception of it.

This prime ministerial archetype, of course, is just as misleading as the national stereotype, and to explain Kevin Rudd's enduring popularity to an international audience – which I have regularly found myself doing over the past three years, as a result of his inflated global profile – it is usually necessary to clear up a few misconceptions about the nation he leads. It is the Australia that Mungo MacCallum affectionately describes: a confounding country of myths, anomalies and contradictions. A place, as Mungo notes, which prides itself on its anti-authoritarianism yet meekly adheres to a bewildering array of rules and regulations. A country with a powerful sentimentalised rural mythology, but which is largely urban and suburban. A welcoming and accommodating land – Mark Twain aptly called it the "cordial nation" – but with an aversion to asylum seekers who head here by boat. A successfully multicultural community prone to racial insensitivity and, on occasions, brute-force racism. A nation where face-paint patriotism has become increasingly fashionable and has been fuelled by a quasi-religious reverence for the Anzac legend, yet which defers still to a British head of state. On the republic, as with other national questions, it is hard to detect any great sense of urgency in dramatically altering the status quo, which speaks of its conservative tradition and recurring constitutional inertia.

Much of Kevin Rudd's success surely stems from his acute understanding of these tensions, and the development of a style of politics that accommodates these contradictions. Thus the prime minister who ended the Pacific Solution has replaced it with an Indian Ocean Solution. (In shades of Britain's New Labour, the slogan "Tough but humane" has become his personal variant of Tony Blair's "Tough on crime, tough on the causes of crime.") The leader in the vanguard of the global climate-change debate has committed his government to what, by international standards, are small reductions in emissions. The man who stood at the shoulder of Barack Obama in Italy to announce the creation of a new carbon capture initiative has also pledged to upgrade and expand the country's coal export facilities. The leader who delivered the national apology for past injustices has preserved the main tenets of the much-hated intervention. The small "r" republican who promised to accelerate the constitutional debate has kept it in neutral. Indeed, for all his frenetic energy and exhausting work ethic, "full speed ahead" has never been his government's catch-cry. His is an administration that prefers to "proceed with caution." But is that not the Australian way? That is clearly his working assumption.

Without question, Kevin Rudd is a man of strong convictions, with a deep-felt and faith-based belief in social justice, but these often remain closeted passions. Because he is such a disciplined pragmatist, he commonly suppresses them in public. Though on the boat-people issue his compassionate impulses seemed occasionally at odds with the political requirements of the moment – his reaction to a direct plea from a beautiful young Sri Lankan asylum-seeker was visibly an arduous test – he had the self-discipline to keep them in check. On the question of the monarchy, his private republicanism is surely a very different construct than his public republicanism. Interviewing him in the run-up to Copenhagen, I left his office after thirty minutes of to-and-fro convinced that the same was true of his environmentalism. He would like to go further, but feels hamstrung by his nation. Perhaps sometimes he privately wishes he *were* a Nordic prime minister.

Yet as well as being highly popular, this passionless brand of politics suits him temperamentally, which gives it an authenticity and, thus, heightened electoral appeal. The "Sorry" speech was a case in point. Placed in the hands of a more expansive politician, with greater theatricality and dramatic range, the script might truly have soared. Instead, it was erudite but strangely impassive. And, of course, very well received. His politics inhabits the same narrow band of self-expression, for he strives constantly for equipoise across a range of issues, and regularly achieves it. Accordingly, a pre-election strategy anchored by the promise of cautious and risk-free change has evolved into a popular governing philosophy. What has emerged is a tacit arrangement with an election-winning majority that he will not propose anything too confronting or unpalatable, and be bound, as Mungo notes, by the social contract hammered out on the anvil of federation.

The oft-heard argument is that this makes Rudd unnecessarily timid. When he sets out to elucidate issues, as with the ETS, it is commonly a defensive ploy. Rarely is he pre-emptive, using set-piece speeches or prime-time interviews to reshape or challenge public opinion – a characteristic of his leadership which became particularly pronounced during last year's boat-people debate. Again, he remains watchful of getting too far in advance of Australian opinion.

Yet, as his near unbroken run of enviable approval ratings attests, Kevin Rudd successfully meets the fairly narrow requirements of his nation: by safeguarding its prosperity, by upholding the fairness doctrine, by delivering occasional, fine-tuned change, by protecting its borders, preserving its traditions and acting appropriately on the country's high holy days, whether at the Australian War Memorial in commemoration of the Anzacs or at the MCG in celebration of the cricket. Were he expected to be charismatic, bold, tactile, funny or handsome, he would doubtless fall short. But that is not demanded of an Australian prime minister, nor considered a requisite for success. Rather than good looks, poise or panache, the physical attribute valued most in a leader is a safe pair of hands. This, after all, is a country that has memorialised its most successful leaders with suburbs rather than stone.

Always worth watching are Kevin Rudd's ritual appearances at the Boxing Day and New Year's tests, for they tend to exhibit many of his leadership traits – the good, the bad and the awkward. Here, his mere attendance demonstrates a respect for tradition along with an understanding of the country's sporting passions, even if he does not wholeheartedly share them. This summer, we witnessed his serious, policy-minded side when he launched an anti-binge-drinking initiative at the MCG. Then, at the SCG, we saw an act of prime ministerial non-compliance, when he punched a couple of inflatable beach balls in playful contravention of the overly officious ground rules. After swotting away a couple of balls, there was a delicious moment of prime ministerial indecision as he weighed whether to retreat to the official decorum of the corporate box, or to stay and play some more. Happily, he was next confronted by a shocking pink beach ball, the trademark colour of breast-cancer research, the quick dispatch of which delighted every constituency.

Whether bantering with Warnie or commentating ball by ball, he demonstrates a functional interest in cricket, although he is politically astute enough never to claim to be an obsessive fan – a falsity that would detract from one of his main selling points, his trustworthiness. Even if his blokeishness on such occasions often comes across as rather strained and staged, Australians forgive him his nerdiness, for it offers proof of his dependability. And who could bemoan his commentary box affability? At least he is having a go. Perhaps they even salute the effort of someone trying so hard to be easy-going and spontaneous. It is Rudd trying to be the Australian everyman, even if he does not quite pull it off.

As for his record of accomplishment, his imprint on Australia has so far been light (although he is not helped here by three-year terms, which have taken on the feel of a perpetual election campaign). Kevin Rudd's most eye-catching achievements have not so much been reforms as correctives. The ratification of the Kyoto Protocol. The end of the Pacific Solution. The national apology to indigenous Australians for past injustices. A second act of national contrition directed at the Forgotten Australians and British child migrants. Had it not been for his government's successful handling of the global financial crisis, an undeniably impressive achievement, his image-makers would have found it difficult to point towards more practical achievements. But, again, would that have truly mattered? For perhaps the biggest thing going in his favour is that nothing has gone badly awry. Indeed, he will go before the Australian people this year touting his credentials not as a bold reformer but a competent managerialist. And a conservative-minded electorate will likely reward him with a second term in office, as it has done with every first-term government since the Depression.

Perhaps one of Kevin Rudd's most lasting achievements, as Mungo suggests, is to have institutionalised Australia's emergent diplomatic influence, a punch that I would humbly suggest has become commensurate with its growing economic and strategic weight. Not only has he nurtured strong bilateral relationships with leaders like Gordon Brown and, in particular, Barack Obama, his new best friend – or NBF in Ruddspeak – he is well on the way to cementing Australia's position in the broader global community through the heightened importance now attached to the G-20. This is an arena in which the prime minister has been genuinely adventurous and bold. In calling for an Asian Union modelled on the European Union, he has even gone in for some flighty rhetoric, and showed so much haste that he failed adequately to prepare the diplomatic ground. So perhaps it should come as little surprise that the foreign realm is an area where he has tested the patience of the electorate and consistently attracted negative headlines for the time spent abroad. People respect Kevin 24/7, but perhaps think that Kevin 747 is getting a bit above himself. Evidently, this is an area where he has gone beyond the unwritten job description for an Australian prime minister, a transgression made all the worse by whispers that his true aim is to embellish his curriculum vitae in preparation for a run at the secretary-generalship of the United Nations.

Outside of sport, has not the Australian preference long been for limited rather than soaring ambition? That may disappoint left-leaning commentators and Labor supporters who yearn for a more awe-inspiring story. But the narrative of the Rudd government is a cautionary tale, and thus runs in happy tandem with the narrative of the nation.

Nick Bryant

Mungo MacCallum

The interesting thing about all the correspondence my essay has provoked is the hugely different ways in which different people see Kevin Rudd. You'd think that after more than three years of watching him in the political headlights some form of consensus would have emerged – or at least two clearly opposing views from the huggers and the haters, which was the case with John Howard.

But although the Rudd-rejecters have come to the more or less unanimous view that the man is all spin and no substance (Greg Melleuish quotes Sir Humphrey Appleby: Rudd is one of those politicians "who engage in activity as a substitute for achievement"), the far more numerous supporters are all over the place. And neither group has so far come up with any convincing explanation for his unprecedented domination of the opinion polls. It has fallen slightly since the advent of Tony Abbott, but it is still at a level most other leaders would kill for – especially towards the end of their first term, when they traditionally experience a slump. If, as Katharine Murphy suggests, we don't actually like Rudd all that much, our approval and respect (and our desire to see him continue in the job) is truly remarkable.

Murphy's contribution is especially welcome because a large part of my essay concerned the Canberra press gallery's failure to come to grips with the Ruddian enigma. Understandably, but disappointingly, the gallery as a whole has ignored the challenge, with the exception of Murphy, who has risen to it in the most flattering terms. But I have to say that I am not convinced by her analysis. She is quite right to say that Rudd is a driven politician, and that he is still very much a work in progress, but neither characteristic is a particularly endearing one; there must be something more to it. Her more "prosaic" explanation for his popularity is that we took a chance by electing him, and that so far he has done nothing much wrong. We feel vindicated and show it by showering him with affection.

Well, yes; but he was streeting Howard in the polls almost from the moment he became leader of the Labor Party; by the time of the election he had been up in the clouds for a year, and even more unusually has stayed there ever since. We certainly didn't think we were taking a chance on him, and if we have spent the last two and a bit years congratulating ourselves on our choice, our backs must be pretty sore from all that patting. If, as Murphy suggests, Rudd still has a lot of running to do before he gets to wherever he is going, we will be in traction by the end of the race. I can't help feeling it is a trifle more complicated than that. And incidentally, I can assure her that Rudd's Australianness does indeed pass the front-bar test – at least at the Billinudgel, "Last of the Good Old Country Pubs," where I spend a certain amount of time.

Greg Melleuish presents the standard view from the Right: Rudd is a professional politician with a lot of experience as an administrator who has done three-fifths of five-eighths of bugger all and very little of that. He acknowledges that Rudd's popularity is "the great puzzle of contemporary Australian politics" and then ignores it for the rest of his comment. Rudd, he says, is simply following the pattern set by John Howard and Bob Carr; but neither of those two ever approached Rudd's longstanding supremacy in the opinion polls. Melleuish goes on to claim that Carr "may be regarded as Rudd's role model." Really? By whom? Unlike Rudd, who worked as a cleaner, diplomat and public servant before entering parliament, Carr (like Howard) really was a professional politician; apart from a brief stint in journalism (political, of course) he knew nothing else. And Carr (again like Howard) eventually did fall into the pattern of believing that winning elections was all that really mattered. No one with even the slightest acquaintance with Rudd would put him in that category: whatever his faults, Rudd is committed to real change and is ruthlessly determined about getting things done. Just ask his staff.

Tim Soutphommasane argues that Tony Abbott is far more culturally authentic than Rudd, and certainly he plays the part, from the budgie-smugglers to the plain-speaking slang: the science of climate change, you will recall, is crap. And Soutphommasane holds Paul Keating up as a model of cultural nationalism – but hang on, is this the Keating who listened to the music of Gustav Mahler, collected antique French clocks and described Australia as the arse-end of the earth? For my money the problem with both Abbott and Keating is that they talk the talk, but their inner selves are very different. The voters eventually woke up to the bipolar qualities of Keating, and I suspect they are already doing so in the case of Abbott.

The fire-fighting, surf life-saving, cycling, gloriously hairy he-man so beloved of Janet Albrechtsen in fact conceals a confused, even tortured personality torn between the sacred and the secular and not really sure how to deal with either. Rudd's cultural attachments are both more subtle and more deeply engrained. Soutphommasane fears that they might actually inhibit him from becoming a "transforming" prime minister, that any truly radical reform would go against his need to be culturally reassuring. I think he is wrong: I detect that Rudd has the true fire in his belly. And in any case, his still inexplicable popularity will encourage him to take a few risks.

Dennis Glover is a Labor insider, but clearly not a huge fan of the present government; like many of us, he looks back with nostalgia on the roller-coaster Whitlam and Keating years. But in this context it is worth noting that the ultimate Labor insider, the man who put the Caw in Calwell, the Wit in Whitlam, the Rah in Wran, the Haw in Hawke, and the Uh in Unsworth, Graham Freudenberg, puts Rudd squarely in the best Australian Labor tradition. I spoke to him shortly after writing the essay but before he had read it, and he had nothing but contempt for those who saw Rudd as wish-washy in his approach. It was, he said, a matter of priorities and timing. Wait for it. Glover, by contrast, sees Rudd as a product of the leftist think-tanks formed after the defeat of 2004. These may certainly have contributed to Rudd's strategy as he targeted first the leadership and then the Lodge, but I am convinced that his roots are planted far more deeply. Once again, his popularity would hardly be so enduring if they were not.

David McKnight would dispute this; from his position on the ideological Left, it appears that Rudd has moved too far to the Right, and that the ideas of the prototype liberal economist Adam Smith have become the basis of his socio-economic philosophy. Certainly Rudd has rejected outright socialism in favour of a regulated economy based around the market, but then, so has every other social-democratic leader in the industrialised world. But as McKnight says, "ultimately Rudd's popularity will depend on voters' instincts about his ethical vision, about social justice and about fairness – the values underlying what's best in the Australian tradition." I am sure it will, it does and it has; this deep-seated connection is the basis of Rudd's appeal.

This and, as Nick Bryant identifies, the belief that Rudd is a safe pair of hands. Bryant, as an outsider, sees Australia as not demanding much from its leaders; as long as they meet a fairly narrow range of requirements they will be accepted. Accepted, yes, but not overwhelmingly popular, as Rudd has become. This implies something more profound, perhaps the qualities that Greg Melleuish sneers at: integrity and trust. It can be argued that Rudd's first term has been something of an anti-climax, without many concrete achievements, although shielding Australia from the worst of the global financial crisis must surely count for something. And it is true, as Bryant notes, that his boldest moves have been in the international arena, where he has been accused of expending too much time and effort.

But in the end it is hard to go past Katharine Murphy's summary: Kevin Rudd is always chasing the future, and will do so while the voters continue to give him the chance. You ain't seen nothing yet.

Mungo MacCallum

Waleed Aly is a lecturer in politics at Monash University. He is a regular commentator for the *Guardian*, the *Australian*, the *Australian Financial Review*, the *Sydney Morning Herald* and the *Age*, as well as ABC Melbourne radio and SBS's *Salam Café*. His book *People Like Us* was published in 2007.

Nick Bryant is the BBC's Sydney correspondent. A former Washington correspondent, he is the author of *The Bystander: John F. Kennedy and the Struggle for Black Equality*.

Dennis Glover has worked as an adviser and speechwriter to several past Labor leaders. His journalism appears in the *Australian* and he is the editor and author of a number of books, including *Orwell's Australia*. He is writing a book on the art of oratory.

Mungo MacCallum is one of Australia's most influential political journalists. In a career spanning more than four decades, he has worked for most of Australia's leading newspapers and magazines and been a journalist and broadcaster for the ABC and SBS. His books include *Mungo: The Man Who Laughs*, *How To Be a Megalomaniac* and *Poll Dancing: The Story of the 2007 Election*.

David McKnight is an associate professor in the arts faculty at the University of New South Wales, the author of *Beyond Right and Left*, and the editor, with Robert Manne, of *Goodbye to All That? On the Failure of Neo-liberalism and the Urgency of Change*.

Greg Melleuish is an associate professor in the school of history and politics at the University of Wollongong. His books include *Cultural Liberalism in Australia* and *The Power of Ideas: Essays on Australian History and Politics*.

Katharine Murphy is national affairs correspondent for the *Age*. She was appointed chief of staff of the *Australian Financial Review*'s Canberra bureau in late 2001 and served in that role for more than three years before joining the *Australian* in 2004.

Tim Soutphommasane is a research fellow at the National Centre for Australian Studies at Monash University and a senior project leader at the Per Capita think-tank. He is the author of *Reclaiming Patriotism: Nation-Building for Australian Progressives*, published in 2009, and worked on Labor's 2007 federal election campaign.

www.ingramcontent.com/pod-product-compliance
Lightning Source LLC
Chambersburg PA
CBHW031400270326
41930CB00015B/3371